Love from Luke 2:
More Lessons, Love & *DOGS!*

By: Melissa A. Sweeney

Love from Luke 2: More Lessons, Love & Dogs!

Copyright @2018 by Melissa A. Sweeney

All rights reserved. No part of this publication may be reproduced, stored in a retrieval system or transmitted in any form or by any means, electronic, mechanical, photocopying, recording or otherwise with the written permission of the publisher Melissa A. Sweeney.

Legal Disclaimer: All names and identifying details have been changed to protect the privacy of individuals. I have recreated events, locales and conversations from my memories of them. In order to maintain their anonymity in some instances I have changed the names of individuals and places, I may have changed identifying characteristics and details such as physical properties, occupations and places of residence.

Legal Disclaimer The information in this book is meant to supplement, not replace proper dog training. The author advises readers to take full responsibility for their safety and safety of their dogs with certified trainers.

ISBN-13: 978-1-5136-4104-1

Table of Contents

Chapter 1 What Happened Next? 1
    Faith & Loki 9
    Let the New Adventures Begin 11

Chapter 2 My BELOVED Chimayo 13
    Lessons Learned-No Regrets! 18

Chapter 3 Lucy 19
    Transporting Lucy 23
    Y'all are Nuts! 25
    Lessons Learned 27

Chapter 4 Day 1 29

Chapter 5 Lucy's 3 Sons 34

Chapter 6 Life with Lucy 39
    Different Dogs, Different Strategies 46
    Lucy Likes Me... She Really Really Likes Me! 46
    Girlfriends & Peanut Butter 47
    What happened to you? 48

Chapter 7 Spay Day 51

Chapter 8 First Times Can be Scary 54
    This is what happens when you don't Shut Up! 55
    A Few Reasons for Dogs to Bark 56
    Tips to Decrease Barking 56
    Benefits of Spaying & Neutering 59

Chapter 9 Confidence Looks Good on You 61
    Lucy IS the Momma 62
    Lessons Learned from Lucy 63
        Giving & Receiving 63

Healing & Trust 65

Chapter 10 The Littlest Peanut **65**

    One Lucky Dog 71

    Where's my son? 72

    Let's get Better Together 73

    Mocho-Man is Back 74

    Sit-Stay-Hide 76

    Lucky gets Lucky 77

    Lessons Learned 79

        It Takes a Village 79

Chapter 11 Hunter **80**

    A Home for Hunter 82

    Dogs- Feel, Love & Have Souls 83

    Is this Bearable? 85

    Lessons Learned 89

Chapter 12 Logan **90**

    Logan gets a Home 94

    Luke, Is that you? 95

Chapter 13 Really Logan-Really! **99**

    Why me! Why NOT me! 102

    Don't Mess with Logan 105

Chapter 14 Luna **108**

    #savethepups! 109

    Strong & Shiny 110

    Adopting a Pure Bred 120

    Dog Breeding 121

Chapter 15 More Friends, More Fun **123**

    Give me Grace 124

Chapter 16 Hello Again **127**

Chapter 17 From Bad to Worse **141**
    Luna- Your name means strong 143
    Refusing to say Abuse 144
    Neglect 144
    Recognizing Symptoms of Abuse 145

Chapter 18 An Angel & a Devil on my Shoulder **147**
    Stronger Each Day 149
    Let Sleeping Dogs Lie 153
    I want to Forgive & Forget…All about you! 156

Chapter 19 Adam **161**
    Adam's Love Story 163

Chapter 20 On Our Knees **171**

Chapter 21 Where God Guides, God Provides **178**
    Lessons Learned 182
        The Importance of Self-Care 182
        Vetting & Money Saving Tips 183

Chapter 22 Let's Go Luna-Let's Go! **186**

Chapter 23 When you Gotta Go-You Gotta Go! **191**
    Farewell my Friends 195
    Lucy's Home 198
    A Turn for the Worse 199
    Bye-Bye Bayshore 201
    A Homecoming 202

Chapter 24 The Road to Recovery **205**
    You own a Business, Silly! 207

Chapter 25 That was Then, This is Now **210**
    God Spoke, I didn't Listen 213

Chapter 26 Love from Luke Dog Sanctuary **216**
    Keep Going, Regardless 218

Lessons Learned..220
Chapter 27 Life Today..**224**
    Why do your dog's exist? 224
    Furever Home...226
    Chimayo..226
    Lucy..227
    Luna...228
    Logan 229
    Me..231
    AND THE ANGELS CRIED WITH US................................232

Preface

Two years ago, when I wrote the book: *Love from Luke: Lessons Learned from a Rescued Dog* my goal was to encourage individuals who adopted dogs with abusive pasts, that there is hope for everyone involved. Regardless of how stressful the present situation is, there is still the promise of a wonderful future with fun-loving memories to make.

Let's face it, many of our lives whether we want them to or not have become a complete façade of our true-selves since the rise of social media. Individuals feel compelled to make posts about their lives that make onlookers think they have a perfect, stress-free life, and are happy. I am guilty of this myself, in a way. Although, I do my best to monitor what goes on my social media pages, I post pictures of my dog's transformation. If the animal abuse is not too graphic, I will post a few pictures of what the dog looked like when they first arrived at my home. Then I post a ton of photos celebrating the dog's first smile, wagging their tail and their first taste of happiness.

Yet, these pictures make it appear that caring for a dog is extremely easy. I find it personally rewarding, and about 90% of the time I am happy in dog rescue. I received extremely positive feedback from my first book. Much to my surprise readers had more questions about my personal transition into rescue than the dogs I was caring for. In this new book, I do my best to explain how the experiences with my dogs have changed who I am as a person over the past four years.

The day Luke passed away was the same day I started to write my first dog rescue book in his honor. I was surprised how much I was actually able to write, with the tears of his loss were streaming down my cheeks. The day after Luke passed away, I took off from work to grieve. The following day, I returned to the research project I needed to finalize, but I felt awful. I texted a friend in Philadelphia, and asked if I could call her. She said, "Yes."

I went into my car to talk to her. I told her I felt weird, I was sad, but could not define exactly what I was feeling. This made me even more confused with what was going on with me emotionally. My friend said, "Melissa, stop talking, close your eyes and take a deep breath. I am going to count to myself silently and then ask you some questions."

I did exactly what my friend advised. Surprisingly, I was able to clear my mind. Calmly, she said, "Melissa, what do you want?"

Without hesitation I blurted out, "I want to write a book about Luke. I want to help people understand the importance of animal and human well-being."

I was shocked by my fast response. In a supportive voice my friend said, "Okay, there you have it. You know exactly what you want. Now, you need to make this happen."

As time progressed, I drifted away from finishing Luke's book. I took on a few more contractual projects. Until the day after my 40th birthday, when I woke in the morning feeling incomplete, a strange sense of lack of accomplishments. The feeling was bizarre and it surprised me. It did not make sense for me to feel so empty, I went into my home office, sat at my desk and looked around. I had dogs playfully running in and out with smiles on their faces wanting attention. Watching them happily play made me realize I needed to finish the book I had started six months prior.

Once I grasped this, I dedicated the next three months to diligently completing the book I started for Luke. I announced the release date to hold myself accountable. I was determined to have Luke's book released on what would have been his 13th birthday, and the goal was accomplished.

I was supported by friends and family regarding my desire to release my first dog rescue book. I explained that I did not understand why it had to be written, but followed the urge in my gut to share what Luke taught me. At the end of the book, I proclaimed that dog rescue was my true calling. However, although I stated this, my proclamation had not fully sunk in. I went back and forth with my desire to have a safe and weekly paycheck or take a further risk and focus on raising awareness about animal and human well-being.

This book explains the heartache and successes of the dogs that have stayed at my home. It also shares my own despair, confusion, and at times the painstaking spiritual and career transformation, I went through after the release of the first book. This is different from anything I have previously released. I am honest and opened about my life besides working with dogs. Being an introvert, sharing this much of myself is hard for me. Yet, after a great deal of quiet time in reflection, I felt this part of my story should to be heard. I have taken into consideration how often I am asked details about it. Most commonly, Was it easy? How did you do? What made you make such a drastic change?

Besides questions, I also receive assumptions that my career change was cliché, the typical story of a person who made money in their field. Then walked away, while giving the corporate life and the suits, the middle finger, claiming they have now found enlightenment.

This is far from the truth. The hardest part of the transition was the support I lost and harsh words I received while I was trying to figure out exactly what was going on.

I frequently use the hashtag keeping it real on social media. So this is me, being honest, real and raw to the reader. My new goal is to also help others going through career transition, and to share the truth about what I went through when learning to step-up and answer the calling that was placed on my heart since I was a child.

Acknowledgments

To all the abused dogs that never got to know true love from a human. It is to honor the dogs that have been returned or sent to a kill shelter to be euthanized because the people who adopted them did not properly dedicate the time to help the dogs overcome their past abuse. This book is dedicated to all individuals who have rescued an animal and provided them with patience, kindness, love, and trust. To Luke, my senior rescue dog, who came into my life, and made me a more understanding and compassionate person. To my mother who taught me at a very young age, God gave us animals to teach us how to be kindhearted to one another.

Dedication
In loving memory of my dear friend, leader and mentor Lori
- Thank you!
Ephesians 3:20
Galatians 5:22-23

Chapter 1

What Happened Next?

On July 23, 2016, I released my first animal rescue book *Love from Luke: Lessons Learned from a Rescued Dog*. The release date was important to me because it was Luke's birthday. This was my birthday present to my beloved Luke, my way of honoring all he had taught me about dog rescue during his brief 18 months with me.

Since the launch of the book, my life has changed in many ways. In fact, my life is far different than what I ever could have imagined it would be. I still have my dog Chimayo, who is my very best friend and is remarkably patient and tolerant of my compassion for all animals. In my heart, I think he feels he is the coolest dog because he is my oldest friend. He was there first, and nothing about my bond with him will ever change. Every day I tell him he is my number one for being so kind and amazing. He allows other dogs to come into our home who are not as fortunate as him. I think Chimayo silently gets annoyed at times. I can tell by the looks he gives me. I cannot put into words how much I love Chimayo. He deserves a great deal of credit for how patient he is with me.

I have become a foster home (foster dog mom) to dogs in need of physical and/or emotional healing (sometimes both) before they can go into their loving forever home or "fur-ever home," as joked about within the animal rescue community.

I am blessed to have kept my old group of friends, who completely understood my decision to keep Luke. I have made supportive new friends active in animal rescue and well-being too. These *animal heroes* or *earth angels*, as I often refer to them as, have also chosen to help disheartened dogs find the true meaning of love.

One of the most amazing women I have had the privilege of getting to know better and whom I look toward as a role model and mentor is Ellie. Ellie was the first person I spoke with when everyone who loved Luke wanted to do something in his honor. I remember the first conversation I had with her. I explained my goal is to someday have my own rescue and dog sanctuary. How I want a lot of land, so I can walk into the kill shelters, and pull all the dogs off death row. Then I will get them proper medical treatment, and shower them with love and compassion. When the dogs are ready, I will then find them suitable, loving forever homes. As one dog gets adopted, another dog will be taken in to save as many as possible. Ellie said "Wow," and commended me for my dedication to animal rescue at my age.

Looking back I feel beyond foolish having boasted at my ambitiousness while having one senior dog in my house. Ellie was praising me while she had a modest 12 rescued dogs in her care! That's right, 12 rescue dogs in her home, as soon as one leaves she volunteers to take in another. At one point since we have become friends, Ellie had 15 dogs, and 10 of them were puppies. In 2016, she found over 30 dogs loving forever homes.

Ellie has had a few articles written about her commendable kindness, dedication, and love toward abused dogs. In all honesty, I do not know of any word that truly applauds the level of compassion she has toward the abused, neglected and unloved. I know wholeheartedly my friendship with Ellie was pure divine intervention. I am thankful to have her as one of my mentors, especially when I feel overwhelmed.

Another new friend I made was John. We have not met in person yet, but I will be sharing how our lives intertwined through dog rescue. John's compassion and dedication to rescuing dogs is insurmountable. He has been involved with over 600 German Shepherd rescues.

Another amazing woman I have become friends with is my mentor Lori. She is the founder of one of the rescues I volunteer with. Lori makes me laugh, she is known for being a little rough around the edges, because she has a keen sense of intuition, she will call a spade, a spade regardless of the reaction back. At times this can be admirable, but it's no fun to be on the receiving end of the insult. Lori puts the dogs' well-being first and foremost. She has taught me that there is always hope and has saved dogs that others have deemed unadoptable or not worth saving. Lori's rescue has grown to gain national recognition finding over 5,000 dogs loving forever homes. In the rescue community, she is an inspiration to many.

Before meeting Ellie, Lori and other new friends I thought I was crazy for having to separate Luke and Chimayo, but I was thrilled to learn I am not alone in this. It is now common for me to hear rescuers give instructions to others helping them as to what dog goes to what part of the yard and when. Then they explain which dogs play nicely with one another and which dogs need to be separated. We laugh about the things we do for these dogs and understand that although it is ridiculous to others, we are doing our very best to give these dogs love and support during their transitions.

There are days that drag me away from caring for my dogs, the way I personally want to. I do have other responsibilities besides rescuing dogs. On stressful days, I remind myself that their worst day with me, would be considered their best day in their old life. One of the new lessons I have learned.

I have received incredibly supportive and positive feedback from Luke's book, as well as negative comments. Yet, these opinions and viewpoints received go with the territory of publishing a book. At this point in my life, I do my best to focus on the achievements versus the disappointments. This is not always easy, but I am working on it.

Love from Luke: Lessons Learned from a Rescue Dogs explains the love and goodness I received from a neglected dog. As well as the frustration and confusion that occurred when we first met. I decided to place a part of my life in the public's hands; therefore I made myself subjective to public opinion. That is why so many individuals can offer public feedback on close to anything on the internet nowadays.

I have received comments such as:

"I love my rescued dog more than ever since learning about Luke."

"I learned more than I thought about working with my rescued dogs, it reminds me to step back when times get hard."

"I never thought to place myself in the dogs' shoes before reading *Love from Luke*, now that I have my dogs' struggles seem more sensible."

Lastly, my personal favorite, "I do not have any animals, but after reading *Love from Luke,* I realized how to be a more compassionate person. I think everyone should read it, it will make you a better person!"

Yet, as I said along with the positives I have received negative comments. Fortunately, they are few and far between. My personal favorite was a man telling me I was really weird and a little freaky for writing a book about a dog. Well, I already knew I was weird, and I don't consider it a bad thing!

The second negative experience turned into a great day of book sales, raising further awareness about how to work with abused dogs. I was selling my book at a local artist event. A man came to my booth, had a conversation with me (not about rescue, but random things about his day) he then took my card and left with his wife. When I went outside, I saw him with my business card mocking the book. Stating that *going to a pound and paying a $20.00 adoption fee is not real rescue. A real rescuer goes into a burning building to get a dog out.* He loudly stated that *people who take dogs from pounds should not call themselves rescuers, and writers should not be considered artists.*

Ironically, I am happy to announce his bad publicity brought many animal lovers, both dog and cat alike, to my table. It was one of my best onsite promotions to this day! Hence, the saying *there is no such thing as bad publicity*.

The most popular question I get asked is; *Does being an animal rescuer break your heart?*

Overall, being active in animal rescue has restored my faith in humanity. It has shown me that many people do have good intentions. I feel that if I allow my anger toward the abuse I have witnessed to negatively impact me I have let the abuser win! In a weird sense, it is a fight between good and evil. Random acts of kindness, although small can have progressive impacts, we may never see them grow, but because of faith, we know a positive difference was made.

I have lost count of how many animals I have seen find loving forever homes. I have had many pet parents show great appreciation for fostering their new furry family member. With social media, I am able to keep in touch with a few of them.

Yet, as you continue reading about my new experiences in dog rescue, I will explain how my beliefs were immensely tested. This experience placed me on my knees in prayer, meditation, tears, and anger. For months I begged God to rid me of these emotions and not personally seek vengeance on the man who hurt one my dogs.

***

A popular comment I receive is: *I could never foster because I would get too attached and not want to give up the dog or cat.*

I specifically choose to work with dog rescue groups that do background checks on the people adopting the dog or cat from me. The applicant provides vet references, personal references, landlords are contacted if they rent versus own a home, and home visits are conducted.

Many people complain about the home visits, but this is important to ensure the dog will actually be placed in the loving home the applicant states they have. One time an applicant wanted to adopt a large German Shepherd for her son. It looked like a match made in heaven. Both the boy and dog instantly connected. The boy took the dog for a few walks during a rescue Meet & Greet. When the shepherd went back into his crate, he sat there smiling. He was listening to the conversation about a possible adoption for him. I know dogs understand everything we say. After the family left, he was a little sad, but the rescue group was ecstatic. We really thought this guy would be in his new home within the next week.

Unfortunately, that was not the case. The applicant lied on the adoption form, she said her female cocker spaniel was fixed. When the home visit was conducted, and the vet was called it was learned they were breeding her cocker spaniel and the owner did not plan on spaying her.

The boy did not get the dog because it would have been an unfair situation for both dogs. Even though the German Shepherd was neutered, he would still be attracted to the cocker spaniel when she went into heat. Spay or neutering prevents breeding, it does not prevent horny dogs from getting it on!

***

As well as receiving good and bad feedback, I get asked many questions about my life after Luke. The most common ones are:

What are you (Melissa) up to now?

What about the wolf and his girlfriend poodle Faith?

How's Chimayo?

What happened to Lucy?

What happened to Lucy's puppies?

Are there other dogs?

I will answer what I am up to first. Let me tell since *Love from Luke: Lessons Learned from a Rescued Dog* was published my dogs, and I travel in luxury wherever we go. I have a team to care for my dogs while am at book signings. I am fortunate enough that the host of the book signings, treat my dogs and I to five-star hotels, and we take a limo almost everywhere we go.

Just kidding!!! That is the complete opposite of my current life.

My book was embraced in the animal rescue community. Most importantly it helped educate people on how to work with previously abused dogs. It is hard to make a lot of money in dog rescue, it goes to our dogs' medical. It is also difficult to receive fame from writing. I do both of these things simply because I love them.

I know animal rescue is my life's calling. My personal transition coming from a research and education background to helping animals full time had many moments of fear, frustration, confusion, and disappointments. I have also experienced joy in its purest form. These moments help me to keep going.

I have become less of Type A personality, it is possible. I have become more adaptable to change than I ever could have imagined. One night my friends and I were going out, but I needed to feed my dogs first. I bumped into my friend, and the dog food flew all over the floor. I just rolled my eyes and shrugged. My friend who remembered the old me started to laugh, I think more at my reaction to the spilled food on the floor. That night my dogs did not eat in bowls, but they did eat. The old me, would have had to sweep, vacuum and mop my kitchen floor before I would have left for a fun evening out.

I would love to confess that I follow my own advice and no longer go into my garage to vent in frustration, but I am still working on that. This does happen a lot less frequently. Mainly because I have learned a great deal more about dogs. I have learned how to respond in a calmer manner in about 85% of surprisingly annoying and/or stressful situations that arise from time to time.

Faith & Loki

My mom's standard poodle Faith and her star-crossed lover, Loki the timber wolf had fun for about another year! Loki was so in love with Faith that he was jumping the fence every time he went outside. If my mother was not home and he was at her house, he would howl the saddest howl by her front door. One day, a neighbor called Dr. Charlie at the clinic to tell him that Loki was howling outside because my mom was out running errands.

Another time, Dr. Charlie came to pick up Loki but he was not ready to go home. He bolted out of the back gate and Faith followed. Both Faith and Loki started running down the street together. My 70-year-old mother started to run after Faith. Dr. Charlie ran into his house and grabbed a slice of bologna. Then he started to run down the street as well, waving bologna in his hand, raised above his head. After about two blocks, my mom and Dr. Charlie caught up with them. Loki wanted to introduce his girlfriend Faith to another dog friend he had in the neighborhood. My mom and Dr. Charlie walked home with Faith and Loki looking disgruntled. But their misbehaving did not stop, Loki had to jump the fence one last time that evening to say good-night to his beloved girlfriend.

I would not be at all surprised if the neighbors have social media video channels, posting what went on between Faith, Loki and the two households living across the street from them. I personally would have moved my barbeque and cocktail parties to my front yard for the free entertainment they consistently provided.

Finally, Dr. Charlie decided that he was going to let Loki out the front door every morning and let him walk over to Faith's house for playtime. However, Dr. Charlie wanted to make sure that this is where his wolf would go. For the first week, he would let Loki out the front door. He would then hide in his bushes, and watch Loki run to my mom's front door. When my mom heard his howl, she would let him in to see Faith.

In the evenings if I was free, I would take Faith and Loki for a walk to prevent them from visiting their other friends. Not everyone appreciated a wolf running through their neighborhood. The walk was always funny. They would get a great deal of attention walking down the street together which they both loved. What was even funnier was when one of them would walk in front of the other and start to strut. They would then look back to see if the other one was checking them out, taking notice to their prideful puffed out chest.

Sadly, Dr. Charlie and his family moved out of our neighborhood, happily on to bigger better things. Although we miss them dearly, everyone but Faith and Loki are happy about their new ventures.

Let the New Adventures Begin

I will do my best to answer the remaining questions. Share the new lessons I learned, and the abundance of love given and received by these very special and unique dogs. I welcome you to join in on my times of joy, laughing until my stomach hurt, love, new friendships, struggles, tears, confusion, anger, stress, my personal awakening, and career transition.

Please remember, while you read about my dogs, there are far too many dogs looking for loving forever homes all over the world. I have been humbled and fortunate to be around selfless individuals such as; Ellie, John, and Lori who have done far more than I can currently do for animals and their well-being. What I am sharing is a small drop in the bucket within the animal rescue community and the lives of rescued dogs.

Let's Go!

Chapter 2

My BELOVED Chimayo

In my previous book, while I was writing the last paragraph, I heard Chimayo loudly puke in the other room, which I needed to clean up. I found the irony hysterical. Chimayo has been my very best friend and consistent support for 14 years. I did not give him as much credit as he deserves in my first book. We have made four cross-country trips together. He was with me the first time I saw the Pacific Ocean and explored new states. He has sat next to me, allowing me to cry in his fur during the most painful and heartbreaking times in my life and has celebrated my grandest achievements with me as well.

He is so kind that one time I had a friend come over crying over a break-up, I left the room to get her a glass of water. When I went to enter the room again, Chimayo was right next to her, and she was giving him a big hug, crying into the side of his furry chest. I quietly backed out of the room and went outside. About an hour later, my friend came outside. With a smile, she said, "Chimayo was truly amazing."

She explained how he just sat there and let her hug him while she cried. It was as if he knew exactly what to do to make her feel better. "Yes," I said, "Chimayo can be very kind and sensitive when the moment calls for it."

Chimayo tolerates me bringing other furry guests into our home. I know he considers some to be annoying crybabies, from the facial expressions and glares he gives me. We have had a few sleepless nights from fosters not being able to settle in when they first arrive.

He has been my protector, and I know he always has my back. Even before having brought other dogs home. Chimayo has always been very protective of me. One time, I thought I left the door to my home open. I wanted to go back to check but my mother said, "Melissa, no one is going to enter your home with Chimayo! God help them if they did."

I have had other people comment that Chimayo is very cute, but they would never enter my home, if I was not there. Personally, I find this comforting.

Along with Chimayo being my best friend, comforter and protector, he is also a major motivation in my life. One of my main reasons for buying a home was I wanted Chimayo to have a yard. He is a red and blue heeler mix, making him a very high energy dog. It is said that it takes a puppy two to three years to mature and become calm. Because of Chimayo, I believe it takes blue and red heelers close to seven years to get rid of their puppy mannerisms.

I have been fortunate enough to work a different schedule and allowed to work from home a great deal of my life. My lunch breaks were able to be spent taking Chimayo on walks or to dog barks before I was able to buy a house. When I would have to leave for work Chimayo, and my sassy little min-pin Dixie (she passed away eight years ago, another of my fur angels) would get very sad. I would tell them that I needed to go to work so I could someday buy them a house with a big backyard.

When I was finally able to purchase my home, only Chimayo was alive, but he was the dog who needed a yard the most. I remember how happy he was when I told him that yard was just for him. It is one of my favorite memories of moving into my home. Taking him from the car into the backyard and saying, "Chimayo, look what I got for you! This is all yours, we finally did it! Remember what I promised."

As soon as Chimayo saw his yard his face lit up, it was the expression of pure joy, and he initiated a game of fetch. We took a break from the game so he could walk the premise of his yard, marking his territory with a big smile and wagging his tail between stops. Once his exploration was complete, he returned to playing fetch. When he came in our house, he stuck his head into each room and settled on his favorite spot in all the places he has been, my bed!

I know I have said this before, but Chimayo really likes to sleep in. I am usually working on my computer by the time he is ready to get up. For the first year, Chimayo would get up with a big smile on his face while he would walk toward his backyard. He sincerely appreciated it and knew it was for him. I wanted Chimayo to have a yard so badly that I even chose a smaller home with a better yard for him. I never knew my yard would be played on my so many other dogs that I have been fortunate enough to help.

One morning, Chimayo awoke and went straight to the back door to play, run and then sunbathe. When he looked outside, the smile disappeared from his face. His ears and tail dropped down, he looked heartbroken. I got up to see what made him look so sad, there were two dogs we had never met playing is his yard and with his toys. He looked up at me with a concerned face almost saying, *I thought this was a very special place for me. Who are they?*

As we watched them play around their ears and heads started to perk up. Someone must have been calling them. Very quickly they ran out of the yard. I watched carefully to see how they got in and out. If they could get in, Chimayo could get out, if he wanted. After work, we went to the hardware store together, to get the needed supplies to fix his fence, in his backyard.

Chimayo also loves the car, and now more than ever appreciates when he gets to be the only dog. I know he misses the days of it being just him and I. Sometimes when my car is stopped, Chimayo will peek his head between the two front seats and kisses my face. I then give his head a kiss in return. One time we were being really silly, and he kept peeking his head between the seats for kisses and to be reminded of how loved he is. When I was ready to start my car I looked over, and saw a couple laughing at how funny we were. I smiled back at them, and their smiles became even bigger. They both gave two thumbs up at the same time. One of them yelled out their window, "Great job!"

Chimayo is smart, I mean really smart. Dog trainers have met him and agree he is one of the most intelligent dogs they have come across. When he was younger and liked other dogs, he competed for obedience. He would win every award there was to win, and he LOVED it! Yet, at home, he refused to practice. I believe he felt it was unnecessary. Only, if my min-pin Dixie wanted to participate, would he obey the commands to get treats too. If she wanted to snooze in her bed, then Chimayo preferred to do the same.

Surprisingly, when we went to training, and it was time for Chimayo to have a turn, he was the best. He walked next to me with such pride, the crowd would oooh and aaah. This pleased him, if he was even half an inch off from stopping to sit when I would quickly change a command, I could see his eyes would look worried. He would look around him to see if anyone else noticed. No one ever did, but that was how important these events were to him. We would drive home with a new toy, a big smile on his face and an even bigger smile if we received a call from a friend wanting to know how Chimayo did. I would change my voice and start to brag in a dog-mom manner.

Chimayo learned how to unlock the car doors and windows, as well as some doors in the house. One time, Loki came over to my car. When he saw Chimayo, he jumped at the window to bark at him. I had the car on, and Chimayo quickly unlocked and rolled down the window. I came running over to my car, yelling in a stern voice, "Do not open that door, no more pressing buttons!"

I got to the car fast enough to prevent a nasty argument between Loki and Chimayo. Someone would have gotten bit. My car window was slowly being brought down. It reminded me of a scene from a crime movie where the criminal confidently and slowly rolls window partly down. The window was coming down low enough for Chimayo to stick his head out and tell Loki exactly what he thought of him in return. Dr. Charlie was able to grab Loki away from the car just in time.

It is comical how Loki and Faith are protective of each other. Loki does not like other male dogs near his main squeeze. Faith feels the same way toward female dogs being around Loki. She can be pretty vocal telling them to stay away from him.

While all this was going on, Jasmine asked my mom, "Does Chimayo knows the buttons in Melissa's car?"

"Oh yes, one time Melissa had to take the car to the shop because he broke the buttons on a road trip. He wanted his head out the window and refused to lift his paw off the buttons for Melissa to put it up."

I could write a whole book on how many memories I have of Chimayo. I love him so much, and as he ages, I sincerely count every day with him a gift. He really is my very best friend!

Lesson Learned – No Regrets!

Chimayo has taught me to slow down. To take at least thirty minutes a day to do something we both love. My goal is to look back at my time with Chimayo with no regrets, only great memories. It is music to my ears when people see pictures of Chimayo, and tell me how happy he looks. It's confirmation I'm doing something right.

Chapter 3

Lucy

Love from Luke ended with me discussing my new foster girl Lucy and her litter of puppies. Lucy, like far too many dogs, was dumped in the Everglades of Florida, also referred to as the Redlands. The dogs cruelly discarded there are forced to fend for themselves. They have to find their own food, shelter from tropical storms and hurricanes. On top of that, they have to sit in horrifically high temperatures, and try not to get eaten by alligators, pythons or get bitten by other poisonous snakes or spiders. As you can imagine these helpless domesticated dogs, live a life of constant fear and stress.

I learned from the Redlands dog rescue group that my Lucy was in the Everglades of Florida for at least five years. She had given birth to several litters of puppies. For years, this rescue group would try to catch her and her other pups but couldn't. Once the puppies stopped coming to the feeding area for nourishment, Lucy would disappear into the woods. She was good at hiding, and the rescue could not find her.

But, leave it to me to fully dive in without a clue of what I am doing except, the compassion in my heart and the faith that somehow it will all work out. Faith the size of a mustard seed, as the good book says.

When I saw the picture of Lucy in the wilderness with a fearful, worried look on her face, I tossed and turned in my bed all night. My mind could not turn off. It was January 11, 2016, Lucy (like far too many dogs) had seven or eight small babies in the chilling swamplands of Florida. What a great meal they would make an alligator or python! What a horrible way for a helpless, innocent puppy to die at the same time.

Facebook photo of Lucy in the Everglades, rescue begging for a foster home

At 3:00 a.m., I got out of bed and went to the computer and completed the application to have Lucy and her puppies come to stay with me. I explained that I had a large garage with a door going into a fenced in backyard. I would heat the garage if needed, and keep the puppies in a playpen. I would do the very best to give what I had to Lucy and her pups. Once I completed the form, I went back to bed, and I was out like a light. Looking back at that night, I learned how important it has become for me to listen and trust my intuition.

At that time, I was confused as to why Lucy was "the dog," I lost sleep over. There are far too many sad stories about animal abuse and animals in need online, but Lucy was the one who stood out in my mind. I still hold dear to my heart my friend telling me, "God assigned you to be Lucy's real-life angel. When you completed the application to assist her, it was because this is who God chose for you to specifically help."

It took me a while to accept this at first. Yet, I now believe this with my whole heart, Lucy and her last set of pups were supposed to be with me. The next day, I heard from the rescue, and they had accepted my application. My main request, as foolish as it may seem, was to call her Lucy, in honor of Luke. The rescuers in the Redlands had called her Phoebe, but they understood the sentiment to change her name. I got off the phone feeling a ton of emotions all at once. I was excited to have my application accepted to be trusted with Lucy and her puppies. I already knew I had signed myself up for a lot of work and an entirely different kind of dog rescue than with Luke. I was happy that I answered the call on my heart to foster Lucy and her pups but that joy only lasted for about five minutes. Then my mind began to race with questions and fear. First came the "what if's."

What if they can't catch her and I got excited for nothing.

What if she doesn't like me!

What if the garage is too cold and I do not have enough blankets and piddle pads.

Piddle pads! Yes, I am going to need A LOT of piddles pads, I just agreed to have EIGHT untrained puppies move in.

How bad will untrained puppies smell up my home?

Is Lucy trained? This could be worse than Luke's peeing problem when he had his kidney infection!

I haven't been around puppies in years, what the heck am I doing!!!

What if I bit off more than I can chew and I will soon have eight to nine dogs howling in my home ALL NIGHT long AGAIN! I know my neighbors are patient with me, but will they be that patient?! My mind then switched over to:

How long would it take for Lucy to like me?

Would she be nice?

Is she aggressive?

What am I to do with an aggressive mother dog protecting her puppies?

Would she let me help her with her puppies?

What if the puppies were already feral?

I had watched a YouTube video of small feral kittens that were only 10 days old.

I had to get myself out of the panic I put myself into, I put on my running shoes, grabbed my headphones, and out I went to the trail close to my home. Exercise helps me to clear my head. I found a place with beautiful scenery by the water. I sat down, my racing mind slowly began to calm down, and my fears disappeared.

I reminded myself of Temperance and her seven kittens. Then I remembered Sonia, another mother cat with eight kittens I had cared for. Plus, the knowledge Luke had left me. This time was going to be much easier, different but easier. I had a team around me. I had even more people encouraging me. I had friends who had experience with mother dogs and their pups who would gladly offer tips and help. My new journey with Lucy and her puppies was going to be completely different from my journey with Luke. This time, I was surrounded by even more wisdom and support than I had been in my past. Therefore, why not take in a homeless mother dog and pups in need of shelter, food, medical help, and most importantly, love!

My soon-to-be journey with Lucy and her pups quickly returned to a positive perspective filled with many adventures, more love, challenges, and greater lessons. I had to remember these challenges would grant me the opportunity to learn more about myself and animals. Looking back, I wanted another Luke experience, which Lucy and her pups did provide.

Transporting Lucy

Three days after my application was approved, I got a call from the rescue, letting me know they were able to catch Lucy and her pups. The team in the Redlands of Florida placed food into a large trap, and the puppies ran in to get it. Lucy followed her pups to ensure their safety and was caught too. Sadly, only three of the puppies had survived. The team looked everywhere for Lucy's other babies, but they were nowhere to be found. God only knows what happened to them in the Everglade swamps.

I was then told that Lucy and her three remaining puppies would be at a vet in Miami Dade for their physical, first set of shots, and to have tests run to ensure they were healthy. Lucy tested positive for heartworm, but that was not a surprise to anyone. I learned the medicine would not hurt the pups she was breastfeeding and that heartworms would not be passed onto them. It was in Lucy's best interest to allow her to have the closest bond possible with her puppies.

About 10 days later, Lucy and the pups were ready to be transported to Tampa, FL. I had organized my garage, posted on social media for friends to please give me their newspapers, old blankets and cleaning products they did not want. I was fortunate to have a friend lend me a 6 by 6 playpen and swimming pool for Lucy and her puppies to stay in. The puppies would always be safe and not harm themselves on anything I kept in my garage.

Another woman and her daughter generously volunteered to drive to and from Miami on the same day to pick up Lucy and the pups. This trip is a minimum of a four-hour drive each way from the Tampa Bay area. We arranged to meet at Ellie's home, closer to where we both lived.

This was it! It was really happening! Lucy, the dog that I tossed and turned all night worried about, was coming to my home. At this point, I was excited to be fully active in rescue again. I was thankful I was able to help and that I was approved to help. It was a relief to know that Lucy and her remaining babies were finally safe. Their lives would be positively changed from this day forward. I was appreciative that I was working with a rescue that allowed the mother dogs to care for and nurture their puppies. Lucy's well-being was just as important as the puppies.

There are many heartbreaking stories of mother dogs giving birth at shelters and rescuers taking the infant pups and leaving the mother in the shelter. To any mother reading this book can you imagine how horrifically heart-wrenching that must be! To make matters even worse, the mother dogs are producing breast milk and become engorged because they do not have their puppies or a breast pump to alleviate this discomfort. These dogs then are in physical pain, scared and depressed. I have been able to help a few mother animals with their young. Hopefully, this book will assist others in understanding the emotions mothers, human or animal, feel toward their young.

Y'all are Nuts!

When I arrived at the meeting place to pick up my new dog pact, it was anything but calm. First, Ellie, whose home we met at, had just returned from a dog rescue event. In the process of getting her foster dogs from the car to the house, one decided to run away and take himself for a walk around the neighborhood. Of course, the rest of us were in a panic mode, running around frantically looking for the escape artist.

I can only imagine what was going through poor Lucy's head at that moment. The woman who transported Lucy kept her in the back of her SUV and had opened the back door to let her out. Lucy sat there, wide-eyed and frozen, watching us chase another dog into their home. Ellie parked her SUV full of large barking dogs right behind the SUV Lucy was in.

Once the dog who ran away was caught and put into the house, it was Lucy's turned to get out of the car she was in, and put her into mine. She was petrified, pulling away with her whole body and forcing us to almost drag her. I had her leash while the other volunteers walked behind her, gently guiding her toward my car. Everyone was speaking to her in calm voices, but she was too scared to care. I am sure she thought we were all nuts. Thankfully, she was on a secure leash. I had brought a bag of dehydrated sweet potatoes (Luke's favorite) to try and coax her into my car, but she was not having it. Lucy could have cared less about them. I think all four volunteers were scared Lucy was going to get away, even worse we feared not being able to catch her if she ran.

While all this chaos was going on, a young girl maybe, 10 years old came over to me and said, "Here," while handing me a shoe box.

I stopped, puzzled for a minute, and said a bit confused, "What is that?" while I simultaneously looked into the box. It was three sleeping puppies. They were the tiniest, sweetest, cutest things I have ever seen. "Thank you," I said.

We were so concerned with getting Lucy into the car, I forgot all about the puppies. The girl had held the shoebox of Lucy's puppies in her lap on the trip back from Miami.

I quickly grabbed the shoebox and showed Lucy her sleeping puppies. She was still terrified. I quickly but gently took each tiny puppy out of the box, and placed them into a laundry basket I had brought lined with some blankets. I pushed the basket with the now awake and crying puppies further into my car, and Lucy got in after them. Lucy's love for her three remaining puppies always has amazed me.

Now, I had Lucy and her pups in my car. I quickly thanked everyone and was off with my new pact.

Lucy's concerned expression on the way to my home

Lessons Learned

The first lesson I learned from Lucy was how important it is to step up and do something when I feel that pull on my heart. The tug on my heart to help Lucy was so strong that I lost sleep over it. Completing the application to foster Lucy has taught me far more than just this.

I believe God places these emotions on all of our hearts. This pull does not have to be for animal rescue, although it is mine. Local communities everywhere are always in need. Take a moment and think about what you are compassionate about. This could be helping the homeless, military veterans, the elderly, children in foster care, the local prison -the list of places in need volunteers is endless. Yet, imagine how improved our communities would be if everyone stepped up and answered the pull on their heart, versus the false belief that their efforts would be too small or insufficient to really matter. As I continue to share my story, I learned how a small act of kindness will gradually create something grander than one could ever imagine!

Chapter 4

Day 1

The ride home was calmer than I imagined it would be. I placed the puppies in the front part of my sports wagon. Lucy sat in the farthest part of the back of my car that she could. She had a worried look on her face, but I think she was trying to look brave for her sons. The last few days had to have been very scary and confusing for her.

Two of the pups instantly fell asleep, stretching themselves out on the fluffy blanket they were given. They could have cared less as to what was going on. The other puppy made it clear that he was the momma's boy in the group, and did his best to climb out of the basket to be close to Lucy. He pulled himself up to look directly at his mother and cried. Lucy just looked at him, but did not attempt to get him out of the basket and bring him to her. This made his cry louder.

When the puppy stopped crying, the smell of poop wafted through the car. I pulled into a local shopping plaza, got out of the car and picked up the puppy that was awake. I took him to the grass to see if he had to go to the bathroom, or if he did everything he needed to in the laundry basket. It appeared he was good, so I placed him back in the basket. As soon as he was in there, he pulled his body back up to peak out, and cried at his mother again.

I asked my mom if she would hold him until we made it home. She instantly agreed, as loud and as whiny as he was, he was still adorable. I placed the small puppy on her lap, he climbed up to her chin and nestled himself into her neck and sweatshirt. My mother started gently petting him, and he fell asleep within seconds. She explained that when I took the puppy out of the car to go to the bathroom, Lucy instantly became alert, lifting her head and moving around to see what I was doing with her baby. Regardless of how scared Lucy was, she remained a protective mother. She was doing her best to trust us, but it was clear she did not have good experiences with humans in the past.

When I arrived home with Lucy, I still had a bit of my Type A, advantageous personality. The garage was ready to go with the donations I had been given. Foolishly, I donated all of Luke's items six weeks before Lucy's arrival. I had a large blue tarp on the floor, a large indoor dog fencing to keep them from wandering too much in my garage, a swimming pool full of blankets, trays to fill with food, water dishes, a dog bed, and I couldn't resist getting them some toys to play with.

I backed my car into the driveway and opened my garage door. I made sure Lucy watched me take her puppies out, and place them inside the swimming pool. I was successful in having her eyes actively follow what I was doing with her pups. I then opened my hatchback, and grabbed Lucy's leash, she instantly jumped out of the car to get into the garage to be with her pups. I was relieved, getting her out of the car was much easier than getting her into it.

I quickly shut the garage door and started to set everyone up with food and water. All of the puppies were wide awake, the vet estimated they were between three and four weeks old, so they tired quickly. Everyone was hungry, so they gathered themselves around the large bowl of food. The smallest pup climbed right into the dish and started to eat – it was so cute.

Peanut in the food dish

All the pups ate the food and drank the water without hesitation. They were young, trusting and innocent. But poor Lucy sat frozen in the swimming pool, watching the puppies eat and carefully observing my interactions with them. They were too little to get in and out of the swimming pool themselves, so they needed my assistance. When the puppies finished their meal, I placed them in the pool to sleep with Lucy.

I went into the kitchen and made a special bowl of food for Lucy with bits of chicken and hotdog. I heated it in the microwave so she would be able to smell the goodness, then I mixed it in with some dry food. When I brought it into the garage, she perked her head and ears up. She allowed me to get very close to her while she ate from the bowl. I was overly excited about this and went back into the house and made her another hot dog. I had bought these as a special treat for Lucy. This time I had her eat it from my hand. She gobbled every piece up and looked for more. I was so excited I got her one more half of a hotdog.

I wanted Lucy to trust and love me so badly, that I introduced her to foods she was not used to eating too soon. The rest of the day the puppies slept, played and did their business on the piddle pads. Much to my surprise, Lucy got up from where she was sleeping and went to the door for me to let her in my yard to go to the bathroom. This behavior made it clear that at one time she was an inside dog. I will never know how she went from being an indoor dog to surviving five years in the Everglades of Florida.

Things were going great, everyone was being quiet, and Chimayo did not seem to care that there were new dogs in the house. He is confident about the role he played in my life. At this point, he still wasn't really sharing his home with them. They were in the garage.

Considering things were going smoother than I could have imagined, I decided to meet up with my friends for a bit. I was gone for about four hours. When I came home, my house was surprisingly quiet. I went into the garage to check on the little family. The pups were all sound asleep snuggled into their mother, but Lucy did not look good at all. She had a strange look on her face, was panting heavily, and was a bit bloated.

My first thought was something inside her stomach had burst. I stood looking at her wide-eyed, not sure what to do. I decided to open the door to the garage leading to my backyard and open the garage windows. Maybe it was stuffy, and she needed air. Lucy tried to get up, but she threw up, then she threw up again, and again until I lost count of how many times she vomited.

Fortunately, I gathered the pups up and placed them on a donated dog bed. They stayed sound asleep while Lucy went from vomiting to diarrhea. Once she felt better, she ran outside to finish getting everything out of her system. I felt completely foolish. I wanted Lucy to like me so badly that I overfed her with food that caused her to have an upset stomach. What I should have done earlier that day was give her the same bowl of food that the pups had versus over feeding her hotdogs and chicken.

While Lucy was outside, I grabbed two large trash bag, and gathered up the vomit and poop filled blankets, and put them straight in the garbage. I then sterilized the plastic swimming pool, dried it off and placed clean blankets in it. I had Lucy stay outside for about an hour to make sure she would not get sick on the new blankets. Around 2:00 a.m., I let her back into the house and went to bed.

Overall, my first day as a foster was better than I had expected. I realized I needed to be very careful of what I fed my new dog pact or I would be giving myself extra work.

Chapter 5

Lucy's 3 Sons

As the days progressed, a schedule came together. My mornings would start around 6:00 a.m. Three times a day, I needed to clean the garage, replacing newspapers and piddle pads. Lucy and the boys would play outside while I would mop, disinfect, and deodorize the garage. I had gotten heaters for the garage on the days it was cold, and thankfully did not need to worry about hot Florida temperatures just yet.

I was learning the three puppies' personalities and thinking of names for them. When I would enter the garage, they would all run to me happily wagging their tails. I would get on the floor, and they would climb on me, whimpering to pick them up and cuddle them. It was adorable. Many neighbors and friends came over to see them as well. This was great because they were getting socialized. Lucy was learning that some humans had good intentions. When friends would enter the garage, I would instantly introduce them to Lucy and ask them to say hi to her. Lucy would sit up in the swimming pool to watch how her pups interacted with us. I believe because everything was always kept positive and upbeat, she was okay with babies being shown affection and love by strangers.

I knew Lucy was enjoying staying with me because I would watch her outside in my yard. When she did not think I was looking, she would run around playing, wagging her tail, and smiling. She was also trying to initiate play with her sons, but they were still too little. It must have been such a relief for Lucy not to have to worry about meals, feel safe indoors, and have a fenced in yard preventing predators from harming her remaining three puppies.

Two of her puppies were reddish brown like Lucy, but they had squarer faces identifying them as part of a bully breed; pit bull, bulldog, or boxer maybe. It was still too soon to tell, all I did know was, I loved and cared for them very much. The other puppy was a darker shade of brown, his hair was longer than the other two, and he was twice their size. He looked completely different, and when I first saw him, I wondered if Lucy was his real mom. Maybe he ran in the cage for food and strayed from his real family. Lucy nursed and snuggled him the way she did the other two, so regardless of if he was an actual blood relative, they sincerely loved each other.

I was asked by the rescue to send in their weight. The smallest red puppy weighed 2 pounds 3 ounces, and although he was the smallest, it was clear early on that he wanted to be the *leader* and had no problem standing up for himself. The middle-sized red puppy weighed 3 pounds 6 ounces. This guy was the *follower*. The bigger dark brown puppy weighed in at 4 pounds 6 ounces, whether this puppy wanted to be or not he was the *loner* because he looked different from the two red ones. If he was Lucy's real puppy, he had a different father.

The big hairy dark puppy, I named first. I did my hardest to resist, but I fell head over heels in love with him. The two reddish pups were best friends. They played together, ate together, and stayed close to each other. The dark brown one was always left out. Even while I was in the room, the smaller pups teased and tormented him. Randomly, all three puppies would be playing nicely, and then the two reddish ones would gang up on him and start barking at the dark one. He would cower in the swimming pool and hide his face. They did not seem to care and would continue to simultaneously bark at him.

Naturally, I would pick him up and cuddle him. If I heard them from the other room, I would go into the garage, get the dark one, and nuzzle him in my arms. We would snuggle on the sofa together, and I would play with him one on one because he had no playmates.

I decided that this biggest puppy should be named Logan, another L name to honor Luke. Logan had a calm and gentle personality much like Luke's. He wanted to be loved, and the way he felt such ease in my arms while being carried almost everywhere completely melted my heart. A few of the neighbors said to me, "Melissa, you are keeping that puppy! Every time we see you, you have that puppy in your arms."

"No, I'm not!" I would respond, "I am letting him spend time with me because his siblings pick on him because he looks different from them. I am keeping him with me, so he does not get hurt and feels loved."

The other two pups were also very sweet, but their rejection toward Logan was natural. I spoke with a few other volunteers that explained the puppy who looks different often is the one that would get picked on. These puppies also have a different scent. This explanation allowed me to justify always having Logan in my arms as well.

The two red puppies were a little harder to name. My friends were hoping to adopt the middle-sized puppy (the follower) and wanted to call him Hunter. That name stuck with him. Hunter had a kind heart, he was very gentle. He was the one who cried the entire car ride home. He cuddled with Lucy the most and would give her kisses. If Lucy had a favorite, I think it was him. If the smallest puppy was not around, Hunter would be kind to Logan, and they would play nicely together. Hunter was the first to be potty trained and loved the praise. His whole face and eyes would light up when he was told he did a good job. Many times when the three pups would play outdoors, they would all want to play with the same toy. If Hunter was able to get the toy from his brothers it was apparent from his strut he was proud of himself. His struts would get even bigger if my friends and I cheered for him.

The smallest puppy (the leader), that ate out of the food dish, ended up being called about five different names until he found his forever home. First, I called him Levi to keep the L trend going, but I ended up nicknaming him Peanut because he only weighed two pounds. As Peanuts story progresses, his name was changed to Lucky which was the most appropriate name he could have been given.

Peanut - 2 pounds - The Leader

Hunter - 3 pounds 6 ounces - The Follower

Logan - 4 pounds 6 ounces - The Loner

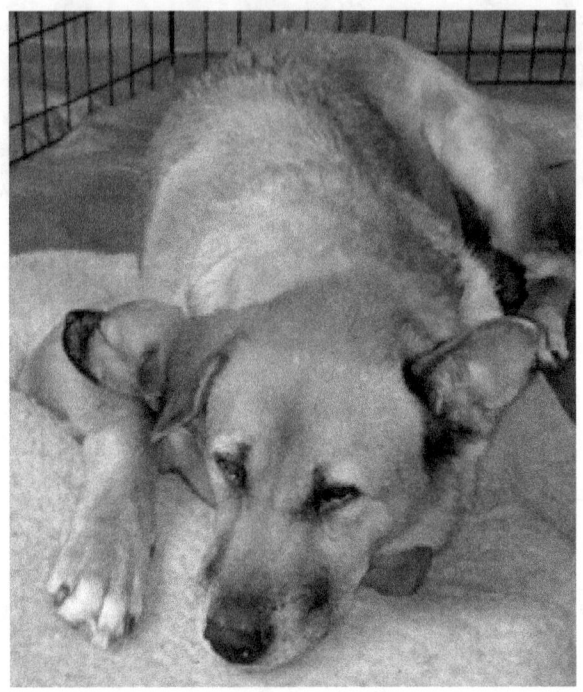

Chapter 6

Life with Lucy

On my 2nd day with Lucy, I attempted to pet her. She allowed me to do so but I think it was because she had her puppies sitting in her arms. My mother took the video, as I pet her back she was wide-eyed and frozen. I decided I would not pet her again until she felt more comfortable. I often wonder if I made the right decision with this. It was clear by how scared she was of my hands moving fast, even when I was bringing her food. She would get a petrified look on her face, put her head down low, and would avoid eye contact. Her body language made it clear she had been physically abused. Yes, hitting an animal is physical abuse, especially when the animal is hit in a fit of rage to intentionally cause them pain.

Lucy loved the food and would walk to my garage door leading to my backyard when she needed to go out. Sometimes she would come in happily on her own. The only reason I knew this was while making a video I caught her on camera prancing into the garage wagging her tail. It's the moments like that, seeing a dog smile, and wag their tail that brings the most joy and reward to the rescuer.

Later on day 2, Lucy was outside with her pups. I caught her go into puppy play position, wag her tail and dance around her pups. They playfully wagged their tails back at her but were still too young to respond. I was so excited I sent all my rescue friends the video of Lucy being puppy like in the yard.

But on Day 3, Lucy went from a playful puppy to rebellious teenager. The day went great, I was actually surprised at how smooth my new routine was going. That evening, I decided to take a yoga class. When I came home my house did not smell good. I checked on Chimayo and he was fine, snoozing in one of his favorite spots in the house. The smell did not seem to bother him.

Oh no! I made Lucy sick again was my first thought as I hurried into the garage. Lucy was comfortably sitting in her swimming pool taking a snooze, while the pups played. When she heard me enter the garage, I could see she was watching my reaction from the corner of my eye. I know my face was shocked, while I fixed the intentionally destroyed items in the garage, I ignored Lucy. I moved the large gate around Lucy and her pups. I said nothing to her, but praised the pups while they got out of my way. Occasionally, I would glance at Lucy and she would stare right back at me, looking me dead in the eye.

Then I took a deep breath and started to evaluate the HUGE DISGUSTING MESS Lucy made on PURPOSE! Lucy opened a large bag in my garage that had my Christmas tree stored in it. I really LOVED my Christmas tree too. It had the fake snow, cardinals, and lights already on it. It was the most beautiful holiday tree I had ever seen and I had admired it for three years. When it finally went on a clearance sale, I called every store within an hour of me, paid for it over the phone and then picked it up. Putting up my tree was my favorite part of prepping for Christmas. For two years it was the tree we decorated for Luke's fundraiser. The year before that everyone decorated the tree while waiting for Thanksgiving dinner to be made. I only had great memories associated with that tree and now it was going to have to be thrown out.

I had no idea what to do with it. Lucy had opened up the tree bag, she actually unzipped it. Then pooped and peed all over my beautiful tree. Then she must have shaken my storage shelf, and the new heaters that I just bought just for them got thrown on top of the messy tree, along with some other items. Then it looked as if she went to the bathroom again on top of those items. What a mess! What heartbreaking mess she made. I really thought I had puppy proofed my garage, but I was wrong. I was mad at myself, mad that I had become overconfident and frustrated that I even left for yoga.

If I opened the garage door, the puppies may get out of their barrier and run into my front yard and the street. I had to then lug the tree and other items through the door leading to the backyard, through the backyard, along the side of my house, then with gloves and old clothes pick up what I could manage and put my beloved tree in the trash.

It seriously looked like I was dragging a body bag out my back gate and trying to jam it into my outside trash bin. In order to do this, I needed to put my trash bin on its side and push the large black bag into it. Then place the trash bin upright and try to close it. I put my full weight on the lid but was unsuccessful. My neighbors, at this point, rarely ask what I am up too anymore, they have accepted my weirdness.

When I got back into the garage I took my phone out and videoed myself sternly telling Lucy that I was very hurt, and confused as to why she ruined my things. She laid in the pool, if she looked away from me, I would tell her to look at me again. She understood what I said and would look toward me. I think she just wanted me to shut up. I told her I knew she did those things on purpose, but we were going to move forward. I wished she could talk, so I could actually know what I did to make her so upset with me. When I started talking to her in my normal voice, her own facial expression relaxed. Her face and eyes became gentle, and her concerned look disappeared.

After that one evening, Lucy never made another mess in the house. When I talked to my friend who is a social worker about it, she said Lucy reminded her of a teenager who went to many different foster homes and would act out to test the newest foster parent to see if they would still keep her.

After that night and my talk with Lucy things went extremely well the majority of the time. Each day she became happier and more trusting. When she thought no one was watching she would run through the backyard with her tail wagging fiercely, she would play by herself and her tail would wag even faster if one of her pups tried to participate. Lucy was beginning to associate me with good and positive things. I was meeting her basic needs for her and her puppies: food, water, and warm shelter. Having a privacy fence where Lucy could only see the yard helped her to feel safe.

By the end of the first week, I had figured out a good schedule for my new foster family. I was usually awoken between 5:00 am to 7:00 am. Sometimes this was due to the pups and sometimes it was because I had family visiting. I would let everyone out in the backyard and would keep the back garage door open. I would then throw out the soiled newspapers, gather their blankets to wash and then disinfect the floor. While floor air dried I would play with the pups or sit and watch Lucy play with them. Chimayo loves to sleep in so while all this was going on he would remain sound asleep in my comfy bed until he felt fully rested.

Once the floor dried, I replenished the food and water dishes, put fresh newspaper on the floor and bedding in the swimming pool. This took about two hours but it was pleasant. I did not like being woken up so early in the morning by yappy puppies, but once I would see the little guys wagging their tails, smiling and clumsily trying to walk toward me my mood instantly changed.

I sporadically had company on and off for the first 6 weeks of the pups' arrival. Once my guests saw Lucy and her sweet puppies, playing in the yard a smile would instantly appear on their faces too. I joke with my friends saying. "My perfect morning starts with my amazing dogs, a strong cup of coffee with some chocolate protein powder thrown in."

After Lucy and her pups entertained my company they would go into the garage, have a hearty breakfast and a relaxing snooze for at least four hours.

Sometimes Lucy would go outside to the bathroom alone. I would watch her hide in the bushes and observe me. Some days she would go in and out of the garage freely. Other days I had a struggle to get her in. I would try to hide in the house and watch her from my window, but if she saw me it would delay her coming in. On days it was cold, the pups needed to have the garage heated for their health. There were days that I would have to chase her through the backyard for her to go inside. This lasted for about three weeks. I was never able to determine what exactly triggered it. Lucy may have wanted more freedom to come and go as she pleased, or she may have wanted a break from her pups.

Yet, this behavior was easy to break when I proved to Lucy, that I was on her side. One evening, one of my male neighbors was outside talking in another language, it was getting dark out and Lucy did not want to go inside. She sat extremely straight by the opened door. If the man started laughing or if his voice got even a slight bit louder Lucy would then begin to sternly bark. She would not budge from the entrance to the garage. This went on for close to two hours. I sat outside with her at a distance to try and comfort her but it was useless. Then my neighbor must have had a friend visit because another male voice started to speak. Lucy moved about 10 feet from the garage and sat closer to the fence in a guarded position. Without much thought, I took the chair I was sitting on and moved it right in front of the part of the fence where the voices were coming from. I looked at Lucy, told her it was all right and went back to playing on my tablet. Lucy stared at me, she was no longer focused on the voices, her physical demeanor changed and she went into the garage to see her pups.

I was so relieved I could finally go to bed. Fortunately, no one complained about me bringing another barking dog into the neighborhood. I also felt that I had gained a little more of Lucy's trust. That she felt secure enough to relax with her pups because I would protect their backyard. It's moments like these where I really wish I could speak dog.

Each day I would try to do something special for Lucy. It was small, but just for her. She was very patient with allowing me to help her with her pups. She never minded if I took one of them into the other room, or if my friends and I played with them. She felt comfortable watching us from her dog bed or comfy pool.

In the morning I would let everyone run into the yard from the garage's back entrance. I would stay inside my house, the pups would run out first and Lucy would walk behind them. I would call her into my house and tempt her with wet dog food that I would only give her. Every day I would place the dog food farther into my home. After eight weeks I was able to get everyone to run through my house into the backyard.

Different Dogs, Different Strategies

Things with Lucy were completely different than with Luke. There had never been a moment when I was able to think, well Luke did it this way. Lucy was different from Luke in every way. Luke craved to be loved; Lucy craved having her basic needs met in a safe environment. My care for Lucy was just as rewarding, and just as important to me as it was with Luke. I found caring for Lucy and her pups less stressful than my first few weeks with Luke.

Luke taught me how to be a more patient person. To relax, laugh things off and not take everything so seriously. This is what I needed to teach Lucy, who lived in constant stress for five years prior to coming to my home. I had to remember that even though things do not always go according to my ideal plan, they get accomplished in a grander way than I could have imagined.

Lucy Likes Me…She Really Really Likes Me!

Puppies grow very quickly and become mischievous. When left unattended I would have the pups placed in a 6ft by 6ft playpen in an area of the garage with their beds, toys, and food. Every so often I noticed my tee-shirts or other items of clothing in their bed. I figured it was the pups getting into things, until I saw it was Lucy!

One day when the pups were outside playing, I walked into the house and saw Lucy in the garage by the washer machine. She was pulling a tee-shirt of the laundry basket and took it into the pool with her. I was very quiet, I did not want to surprise her, Lucy was still skittish, but I was smiling from ear to ear. Then she walked past me into the swimming pool and sat on my tee-shirt. I was so excited I called my friend Roger; I went into the other room and did a silly happy dance while I told him what Lucy just did. Roger was just as excited and said, "Melissa that is huge!"

Helpful Tip

When Lucy wanted to sleep on my clothes it was because she wanted to be close to things that had my scent on it. My pajamas or a tee-shirt I wore during the day had my full odor on it so that is what she wanted to have. This meant my scent offered her comfort. This confirmed Lucy was happy with me as her foster and may possibly even love me.

Many experts recommend when a person has to leave their dog when traveling or for other reasons, they should leave their dog with an old tee-shirt or old pillowcase they slept on the night before. The tee-shirt or pillowcase now has the owner's scent on it, this will help to alleviate stress and anxiety the dog may have because they miss their owner.

Girlfriends & Peanut Butter

Lucy and I had several experiences where I know I had to prove myself as a trustworthy person to her. By the time the pups were eight weeks old they were always in mischief, Lucy appreciated when I would put them in a crate so she could have some quiet time. One day, two of her pups were pulling on her and being very annoying. All of the sudden I heard a snarl; I had never seen Lucy make a mean face, show her teeth or be aggressive in any way, she was always sweet. But this day she completely had it with the pups. When she growled at them they quickly ran away, and hid under the chair I was sitting on. We all looked at Lucy wide-eyed, we had never heard her growl before. When Lucy saw my surprised face, sadly she became afraid of me. With her head and tail down ran right into the garage to hide. I put the pups in their crate, went to my cabinet and got a jar of peanut butter. I then slowly walked into the garage, sat on the floor about two feet away from Lucy and extended the opened jar of peanut butter. She made eye contact with me, I smiled back. She was hesitant but I urged her to indulge. "Trust me, it's a girl thing, and you deserve this," I told her

Lucy quickly relaxed and loved the special treat she was rewarded for having a tough day as a mom. Lucy understood, I would never choose the pups over her, even though I played and carried them around, she was equally valued and loved.

What Happened to You?

I had one other occasion that scared Lucy before everyone got adopted. Around 3:00 a.m., there was a loud bang in the garage. This woke Chimayo up. He quickly jumped out of bed and ran proactively around the house until he realized the noise was coming from the garage. Annoyed, he went back to bed. He really does have a lot of patience so he can be bothered with them from time to time.

When I opened the garage door Lucy ran past me into the backyard faster than I had ever seen her run. The dreadful look on her face really bothered me. I never saw a dog look so fearful, I left her outside, and went into the garage. It looked as if it had snowed. The pups found a paper towel roll and paper toweled my garage. They were delighted with the mess and had no idea what they did was wrong. I gathered them up, let them go outside to the bathroom and then put them in their crate. I did not say anything to Lucy, I just allowed her to watch what I was doing. I could see her from the yard peeking in.

The garage took minutes to clean. Once finished, I grabbed the peanut butter and encouraged her to come back in. Lucy responds well to treats. She slowly and cautiously came back into the garage, got comfortable on her bed and licked the peanut butter off a bone I had for her. My house was quiet again, but I could not get Lucy's scared face out of my head. What had she gone through that she would even leave her puppies to protect herself?

She was a fantastic mother. I had to put these thoughts behind me, reminding an abused dog of their past delays their emotional growth and trust. Another time, a neighbor brought a bag of eight large dog bones to my home for everyone. These bones did not have knots on the ends of them, so they looked like rolled up newspaper. Lucy watched as I opened the bag and let each dog pull out the specific bone they wanted. I then brought the bag over to her so she could pick out her own as well. Lucy hesitated so I pulled the bone out for her. When it was out of the bag I thought she would take it from my hand but she jumped about two feet away from me. She was shaking and looking at me with those wide fearful eyes I hated to see. Calmly, I told her it was okay, put the bone on the ground and rolled it over to her. I got up and left the room. A few minutes later I peeked in and saw Lucy had the bone between her two paws. She was lovingly rubbing her face on it. *Only good things from now on, my sweet Lucy,* sounded in my head when I saw her enjoying it.

Chapter 7

Spay Day

Once the pups were old enough to be weaned from breastfeeding, it was time to get Lucy spayed. The clinic my rescue was working with was about an hour away and I needed to have her there by 7:00 a.m. I woke up a few hours earlier to give her a calming dog pill to decrease her stress levels. After all, each time she would get in a car, she would end up with new people or dumped in the wilderness. I wanted to ease Lucy's stress as much as possible.

At 5:00 a.m., I got myself and Chimayo ready for the day. Then had Lucy and the pups go to the bathroom in the backyard. As the pups playfully stumbled into the garage I gathered them up and placed them in a crate in my car. Then I had to slowly put the leash on Lucy. She was still too afraid to wear a dog collar. I had to slip a loose leash over her head. Once it was on, I would tighten it. I pulled the back of my hatchback as close to the garage door as possible. Then went back into the garage, while holding Lucy's leash I opened the garage door, and Lucy jumped into to the back of my car to ensure her babies were okay.

The trip to the vet was a lot less stressful than the pups' arrival to my home. They were old enough now to appreciate the car ride, and they could see their mother through the crate.

When I got to the spay clinic, I explained how scared Lucy was. They allowed me to pull my car to the back of the building. The doctor and three assistants came to help me get Lucy out of the car. She was petrified; she leaned as close to the interior of my car as possible. Her terror broke my heart. I watched a team of four as they walked Lucy into the clinic. Everyone was speaking in soft, loving voices to her, but her entire body language made it clear we were not comforting her. She had her head drooped down as far as it could go, her tail was down, and her whole body looked almost distorted as if she was trying to suck her head into her body like a turtle. Once she was inside it was okay for me to leave. I yelled in, "I love you, Lucy, I will be back!"

3:00 p.m. could not come quick enough. When it finally did, I packed the pups back into my car and away we went. My mother came for the ride to keep me company. When I arrived at the clinic, I pulled my car to the back of the building. The veterinary team was waiting for me with Lucy. They were trying to get her to walk to my car. I had grabbed her puppy Hunter from the crate and had him in my arms. I was trying to coax her into my car with her pup like I had in the morning. Again, Lucy was terrified. She would not budge and was trying to break free from the leash around her neck. Suddenly, I just stopped participating the in commotion. I handed Hunter to my mom and asked one of the volunteers for the leash. As soon as it was in my hands, I said very directly, "LUCY-come on."

When she heard my voice, she suddenly lifted her head. Once Lucy saw it was me, she calmly walked toward the car with me and jumped in. Lucy coming to me when I called her meant the world to me. It meant she trusted me, and wanted to be with me. She wanted to return home with me to enjoy her life. The ride back was very quiet, the pups were exhausted from watching all the excitement of trying to get their mother into the car. Lucy was exhausted from her operation plus stress. When we got home, I backed the car into my driveway, once again Lucy walked with me into the garage. I kept the leash on her to walk her in the yard later that evening, and lead her to the swimming pool filled with fresh pillows and blankets. Lucy was so relieved to be home she laid right down, before I was even out of the garage she was sound asleep.

Chapter 8

First Times can be Scary

The pups needed to be away from Lucy for at least 48 hours so she could rest and not be injured by their roughhousing. This was hard on them, they could not understand why they were in a new part of my house versus snuggling next to their mom where they usually slept. They whimpered and barked most of the night. Chimayo just looked at me annoyed as if to say. "Way to go, you did it again, only this time you have three crybabies versus one giant baby, ugh!"

This behavior in puppies can be completely natural when they are first adopted and in their new environment. This can also occurs in older dogs that are rescued and in an entirely new home.

If you experience this with your new dog, please remember, that individuals also face social anxiety, fear of change, fear of the unknown, and fear of new events. Our mind can race with worst case scenarios and those dreaded *what ifs*. We have all experienced this many times in our lives. As children having to start a new school, as adults starting a new job, having to relocate, and then not being able to sleep in a new place, because it is different. Let's be completely honest and admit these emotional times just flat out suck! This is what it is often like when a new dog is brought home regardless of their age.

Having learned from my mistakes with Luke and being wide awake, I grabbed my tablet and went into the room I had unsuccessfully put the puppies to bed in. They were happy to see me, as I sat on the floor they clumsily got on and off my lap, climbing up on me and trying to communicate they wanted Mom! The bedroom was not the successful idea I hoped it would be. I placed them in my backyard while I researched how to get them to feel calm and be quiet. They were going to get neutered the following week themselves. Then they would be off to their loving forever homes. I wanted to fix this problem now. Getting them adjusted to not having their mom around was beneficial for them. I understood that in about two weeks my house was going to be quiet again, and I would miss them.

This is what happens when you don't Shut Up!

After conducting the research and applying it to the pups, I posted a blog. I intentionally gave it an alarming title because earlier that week, it was all over the news about how a woman wrapped her dog's mouth up with tape and posted the picture online with the headline *this is what happens when you don't shut up!*

This picture and comment caused an uprising amongst dog lovers all over the nation. The local police department in the lady's community was flooded with phone calls from all the country demanding the woman be arrested for animal abuse. Several animal rescue groups volunteered to take the poor dog in, and many families wanted to adopt the dog to save it from future cruelty.

What became even more heartbreaking during this ordeal was individuals who do not deserve to own dogs started posting pictures of their own dogs with their mouths taped shut, defending the abuse. The positive in this situation was many of these dogs were saved from further torment, found rescues to protect them and help them overcome their past abuse.

Therefore, I felt giving my blog that title was timely and appropriate.

A Few Reasons for Dogs to Bark

- They hear a noise and want to warn you.
- They have anxiety, and their attention needs to be redirected, this will help to decrease their stress.
- They have missed you and want your attention. Especially if your dog spent the day at home alone, waiting for you. Taking a few minutes to give your dog a happy greeting when you return home settles them down quickly. It lets them know you missed them too while you were away.
- They could be sick.

Tips to Decrease Barking

- Find or create puzzle toys to keep the dog entertained. I found a few easy ones online. My personal favorite is getting a cheap ball or toy. Put it in a bowl, fill the bowl with soup broth, and put it in the freezer until frozen. Once the broth has frozen, the dog will lick the flavored broth, trying to get the toy they see at the bottom of the bowl. I keep these in my freezer, and give them to my dogs during hurricanes or when fireworks are going off. They concentrate on getting the treat out of the bowl, and forget about the loud noises outside.

- If your dog is left alone experts recommend leaving a radio on for the dog to hear voices. Many dogs do not like to be alone. Being left alone in silence can increase their anxiety and stress. Hearing talk radio helps to decrease this fear, even if they cannot see who is speaking.
- Ask your vet about different calming supplements that can be put into your dog's water or sprinkled on their food.
- I've personally taught my dogs the command *relax*. When I tell them to relax, they lie on their back and stretch out. I speak in a low voice and pet their stomach. I only pet them very gently with the tips of my fingers. Stroking them with my full hand may confuse them, and they will think I want to play. Having my dogs know this command has made it easier for me, especially when they have a vet appointment. One of my dogs instantly goes into a relax poise, which makes anyone watching laugh.
- Dogs can be trained to learn the command *quiet,* for them to stop barking. To make learning this command a fun bonding experience, the dog can then be taught to *speak*. When they hear the word speak they will respond with a bark. My mother had a male dog that learned to answer when he was asked, "Who's the man?"
- Some find spraying with a water bottle to hush a dog controversial. Having water gently sprayed on their face does surprise them, and will quiet them down momentarily. This is a quick fix if there is a baby or someone sleeping and the

house needs to be quiet. The water should only be sprayed once to surprise them. I tried this with Chimayo, but he thought getting sprayed with the water bottle was fun and wanted me to keep doing it. My friend's dog got sprayed a couple times during training. They stop barking when they see that water bottle. It should only be a mist sprayed, about 18 inches away from the dog's face, and sprayed one time, twice if needed. The spray bottle is not meant to scare or harm the dog.

- If there is something that irritates or excites your dog and causes them to bark, remove that item from the dog's site. I have had dogs that did not like lawn statues. I moved them to where the dogs could not see them, and the barking stopped.
- Tire your dog out. If you need to leave your dog, and you do not want them to bark while you are away, make sure they are tired before you go out. It is not fair to a dog if they are crated all night, get let out to go to the bathroom for five minutes, and then are put back into their crate. Take them for a long walk, run, or play fetch with them. If you do not have a yard, find a local park for them to play at.
- Animal well-being is growing. I know many people have started taking their dogs to puppy camp once or twice a week. I understand that can be expensive; there are dog walkers who can visit your dog during the day to play with and walk them.
- Lastly, when your dog stops barking, praise them. I love to spoil, so I also give my dogs a little treat.

Benefits of Spaying & Neutering

As I shared in my first book, Luke was never neutered. In his senior years, he had perianal gland tumors growing around his anus. These tumors were caused from too much testosterone running through his body. They were pushing his anus out of his body. When he was finally neutered he needed to have the tumors removed as well.

Spaying and neutering prevents overpopulation. I will never understand people who go to breeders for a purebred when rescues are flooded with dogs that were initially purchased from a breeder.

If female dogs and cats that are not spayed there is a high chance, they can develop breast cancer, uterine infection and various other forms of tumors that can also become cancerous. The latest study showed female dogs that are not spayed have a 50% chance of developing one or more than one of these illnesses. What is scarier is 90% of female cats that do not get spayed can develop cancerous tumors as well. That is a pretty high risk level!

As a matter of fact, male dogs that are not neutered are equally at risk of developing prostate and testicular cancer. Early neutering in male dogs prevents them from being aggressive or seeking to be the alpha dog of the house. Because they become calmer after being neutered, their wetting inside the home and around the home to mark their territory may decrease. Plus, male dogs may stop digging holes to escape when they smell a female dog in heat.

Due to the over-population of dogs and cats, local vets and animal rescues groups offer low-cost spay and neutering. The surgery takes a few hours, and your pet is able to return home the same day.

They require a few days of rest, but many owners admit that within 24 hours, it is hard to get their dog to stay still.

I understand there is a heated debate about the best age to spay or neuter a dog. Ideally, it is safest for a male dog 6 months and older. Luke was 12 years old when he was neutered and all his tumors disappeared. However, because over-population is such a problem, rescues will spay and neuter puppies as young as eight weeks old. The surgery does not bother them, and many cities have created laws that the puppy must be fixed before going to their forever home. The vet that first cared for Lucy and her puppies had my rescue legally sign a form that her puppies were to be fixed when they weighed 10 pounds. To save their lives, the forms were signed, and the little guys were, neutered at 10 weeks.

Chapter 9

Confidence Looks Good on You

By April of 2016, Lucy was finally an indoor dog. First, she would only stay in my kitchen on her dog bed as if it was a float in the middle of the ocean. She gained confidence because, as you continued reading, I ended up adopting Logan, the biggest and furriest pup from the litter. If Logan jumped up on the sofa and did not get in trouble, Lucy figured it was okay for her to relax on the couch too. She enjoyed being around people and wanted to be acknowledged when I had friends over. She never allowed them to pet her but would stand behind me or sit up on the sofa when they arrived. Then I would proudly say, "You know my amazing dog, Lucy, right? Isn't she pretty, I love her so much!"

If I did not introduce her, she would stand behind me and whimper until I did. If my friends and I had settled in a room, Lucy would quietly walk in, lay down and make an *umph* sound so we would know she was there. I would calmly say, "Hi Lucy," and return to my guests.

One time, I hosted a birthday party. Everyone was trying not to laugh because Lucy appeared to get a slice of cake. While she was eating it, she got frosting stuck to her nose. I am not sure if she could reach it to get it off, but it was adorable to see her comfortably sit with us while having white and pink frosting on her snout. My friends and family silently giggled because we did not want to make her feel self-conscience.

Another time, my mom came over, and Lucy was relaxing with Logan in the dogs' bedroom. Yes, I did convert one of my guest bedrooms into a room for my dogs. Logan was making a fuss over my mom, and Lucy was waking up from a nap. I went into the room and started praising Lucy for being so pretty and telling her how my mom wanted to see the prettiest girl in the house. Lucy had a big smile on her face, she was soaking in every ounce of praise we had to offer. She started to strut down that hallway into the living room to see my mom when suddenly a KA-BANG-BA-BANG- BANG-BANG sound came echoing through the hallway. Lucy stopped dead in her tracks, turned around and ran right back into the dogs' rooms with her head and tail down.

Frustrated, I asked what that noise was. Her pup Logan, was still in his clumsy stage and fell over his metal dog food bowl. Well, it was almost a very proud moment for Lucy, but since she was finally safe with a good rescue and foster home, I knew there would be more.

Lucy IS the Momma

In all sincerity, there were only a few occasions when Lucy and I butted heads regarding care for the pups. I will be sharing these moments throughout the next few chapters, explaining the uniqueness and cuteness of each of her pups.

One day, Logan fell into the pool. He was shocked, but instantly started to swim. I grabbed him out the pool, and began to dry him off. Lucy stood there watching me and started to whimper. I quickly put him down and pushed him toward her. She picked him up and took him into the garage. I peeked in to see Logan in a state of delight, having his mother and brothers fuss all over him. It was another heartwarming moment reminding me why I'm an animal rescuer.

Lessons Learned from Lucy

Giving and Receiving

As I watch Lucy's confidence grow during her time with me, I understood the importance of being able to accept help from others in times of need. As a society, we have been conditioned to be self-sufficient, that needing something from someone is a sign of weakness, that it is shameful and embarrassing. As I watched Lucy hesitantly accept the gifts I wanted her to have, I acknowledged that I personally was able to accept donations for Lucy, but I could not always receive assistance from others for myself.

As the pups got bigger, I noticed Lucy allowed them to sleep on the dog bed and she would sleep on the cold garage floor. I went to the store and got her a bed, too. It was extra-large, when I placed it on the floor I told her it was just for her. If a puppy got on it, I would pick them up and lay them on the older bed. It took a couple of days, but Lucy started to love her very own bed. I was giddy when I saw her stretched out, snoring on it.

I realized I could personally help others, but I would catch myself denying acts of kindness from others if it was specifically for me. For example, if someone picked up the check when we were out or gave me an expensive gift, I would feel obliged to purchase the next meal or flat out refuse to let them pay for me. I would also feel uncomfortable about the expensive gift if I thought I could not give one of equal value in return. I know I am not alone in the struggle of receiving. A sad reality is, many times the person giving has strings and expectations attached, making it hard to recognize sincerity. I realized how happy I was when I saw Lucy enjoying what I gave her. I understand as a society many individuals need to take their own inch worm steps to accept kindness and blessings others want to give.

It has been clinically proven that the person committing the random act of kindness or generosity receives happiness from giving. The feeling is so good that it actually improves one's health and mental outlook. The compassion can extend to strengthen a community and gives one a sense of belonging. In understanding the larger picture of the benefits of accepting kindness, I am slowly learning to be more open to what others seek to give.

Healing and Trust

Another lesson I have learned from Lucy is that healing from abuse and learning to trust again is different for everyone. Lucy's healing process is much slower than other abused dogs I have met. This does not matter because Lucy has her forever home and is loved very much.

The emotional healing process cannot be rushed. Yet, each small step can be celebrated, and the more we celebrate, the more fun we have while healing.

Now, I think it's about time you got to know Lucy's sons.

Chapter 10
The Littlest Peanut

Peanut, the smallest of the pups, was fierce and bossy, but his smallness made his behavior entertaining. Before Lucy and her sons arrived at my home, Peanut had decided he was going to be the boss. He was a 2-pound spunky little guy who was very vocal about getting his way. It was clear no one was going to push him around. I referred to him as the leader because his brother Hunter would do everything Peanut wanted. Logan, the biggest pup was more laid back would walk away if Peanut started problems with him.

Peanut had a number of names during his stay with me. I originally named him Levi. I had wanted all the pups to have L names in honor of Luke and gave the shortest name to the smallest pup. The name Levi did not even stick a day. The puppy had a round head and body. Plus, he had reddish-brown fur. When he would lie in his food dish, he reminded me of a peanut, and that name stuck.

On the pups' first day with me, Peanut jumped into the food dish, as if it was a dog bed, and started to eat. His brothers stood there and watched, but did not try to move him. I got them another bowl. They allowed Peanut to make feeding time interesting. He would run as fast as he could between the two bowls of food before he decided what one he wanted to lay in for his meal.

Sadly, Peanut would instigate the bullying of his brother Logan for looking and smelling different. When Logan got picked on, I would take him into another room. I believe Peanut was pleased because he got more of his mother's attention.

However, Peanut did have a super sweet side to him as well. He was the first puppy I taught to kiss people on the cheek. After he learned to kiss, Hunter caught on as well. Logan never mastered kiss. I would say "Kiss," and the pups would give whoever was closest to them a peck on the cheek. Everyone found it adorable. I did not have Logan kiss, I tried, but he would open his mouth wide and moved toward the persons face with his teeth showing. It looked like he was going to bite them. Once he grew up, my kiss trick could get him in trouble.

When I would come into the garage, Peanut would jump out of his bed, and run the fastest to greet me, sometimes tripping over himself because of how quickly he was moving to come say "Hi." This made him even cuter. As all puppies do, he loved to be held and told how special he was. Regardless of how pushy he was, it impossible not to fall in love with him.

Peanut was impressed with himself. He was amused at how the other puppies would follow his yappy commands. Hunter would mimic anything Peanut did. Logan would walk away to be left alone. No matter the reaction, Peanut was proud that his yap DID get a reaction. Within the first few days, the pups left Peanut to eat in his own food dish and shared the other bowl together. This was another thing that made Peanut feel important.

One night when I was putting the pups into the gated area of the garage, I slipped on a piddle pad. I had Logan and Peanut in my arms, I fell right on my butt in the middle of the garage. The pups were afraid, Logan ran to his mother to protect him. Peanut got up and started making the most horrific screeching sounds I've ever heard a puppy make. He started walking in circles while his screams got louder. To make this situation worse, Lucy grabbed Hunter and Logan, pushed them behind her and started frantically barking at me. *Great, I was just beginning to earn Lucy's trust, and then I drop her baby on the floor*, I thought to myself. To make matters worse her baby would not stop crying.

In a panic state, I grabbed Peanut and, in my pajamas, drove to Dr. Charlie's house. When I got there, he was out. I texted Jasmine and told her what happened. Jasmine said to sit tight, they were on their way home from a show. I went to my mom's house with Peanut and waited. While I was waiting for Dr. Charlie to come home, I should have gone to my house and changed my clothes. Jasmine's parents and her adult children all went to the show as well. Her whole family got to see me in my pajamas but, they were polite about it. Thankfully, my pajamas are modest, and I have seen people tagged in shopping videos wearing them in public, so I sort of have an excuse for going to my neighbor's house in them.

Dr. Charlie grabbed his medical bag and quickly examined Peanut. He said Peanut had a concussion and needed to take it easy for a few days. I thanked Dr. Charlie for all his help and took Peanut home.

When I opened the garage door, Lucy quickly looked up. I walked in with my head looking down at the ground. I did not want to make eye contact, I wanted her to know she was still in charge of the puppies, and I was being respectful to her. I placed Peanut in the pool and gave him a little push to walk to her. I then put some extra heaters on to make sure the pups would be extra toasty that night. The temperature had dropped down to the 50's. For a Florida dog and puppy, that is cold. For a Floridian, that is cold too. I could tell Lucy was watching me closely the entire time. I had hurt her puppy and possibly betrayed her trust. I walked out of the garage in silence and went to bed.

Things were good for about three days. But then the temperature dropped into the 40's. My garage was too large to be safely heated for Lucy and her pups. I needed to transition Lucy into my house sooner than she was ready for. Her complete transition into my home took four months before she felt comfortable.

My garage was ideal because everyone had plenty of playroom and went directly to my backyard. Everyone was going to have a smaller but warmer room. Lucy wanted no part in this. She kept running outside and hiding. Then the puppies would start crying for her to return to them. They were very young and felt the safest with their mother. What I did not realize was Lucy carried Peanut outside and hid him in the bushes to protect him from me. After all, I did drop him on his head, then made him cry the worst cries I have ever heard. In the midst of his hysterical crying, I grabbed him and ran away with him for what probably seemed like forever to poor Lucy. Naturally, she did not trust me around her puppies, especially her smallest.

When I found him and brought him inside, he did not look right. His eyes were watering; he was lifeless and made horrible gasping sounds when he tried to breathe. It reminded me of an old man who had smoked his entire life and would gag when he tried to talk from so much lung damage. I knew Lucy would lose even more trust in me, but I took Peanut to Dr. Charlie's house again.

Dr. Charlie was not happy with me when he saw Peanut. I explained that I kept him warm, but had let him outside to go to the bathroom. When I brought him in, Lucy would carry him outside again to protect him from me. Poor little Peanut was diagnosed with pneumonia. Jasmine told her daughter to get her nebulizer, used for asthma patients. She held little Peanut in her arms and gave him a breathing treatment. They gave me a small crate and bedding for him. I was told to give him a nebulizer treatment every two hours. Jasmine said to bring him back in the morning. She was going to take him to the veterinary clinic to be examined. I came home with Peanut but did not allow Lucy or his brothers to see him. I had them in a spare bedroom, they were quiet, and I did not want to disturb them.

I was up with Peanut every two hours, giving him a nebulizer treatment as instructed. It was so scary watching this two-pound puppy gasping for breath in my arms. He wanted to be comfortable but could not find a position he wanted to lay in for too long. As I tried to console him, I had tears streaming down my face. I would pray to God, asking him to heal the puppy. Then I would tell Peanut in a sad voice, "You need to stay strong, you HAVE TO GET BETTER, you can beat this!"

Luke had only passed away four months prior. I was rocking Peanut in my arms, thinking I made the wrong choice in fostering. Allowing the worst *what if* thoughts to blaze through my mind, while I watched this tiny puppy fight and gasp for each breath. I blamed and hated myself. Clearly, I was unqualified to properly care for a mother dog and her pups.

Around 4:00 a.m., Peanut finally settled down. I put in him his crate surrounded by stuffed animals that I had to search for in my house. I realized that he was used to sleeping with his siblings and sleeping without them felt weird. Probably as strange as when a person needs to sleep in a new place, the first few nights may take some getting used to. Peanut cuddled in with the stuffed animals. He started to relax, and his breathing got a slight bit better. I slept on the sofa with his crate placed on the ottoman next to me. If he needed me, I would hear him. We slept for three hours. At 7:00 a.m., Lucy and her pups were awake, they wanted breakfast and to go to the bathroom. Chimayo sensed little Peanut was sick and wanted to stay away from him. He decided to relax in his bed for a few more hours.

One Lucky Dog

While Lucy and the pups were out, I put Peanut in the other room. He had made it through the night. He was sleeping but his breathing was still a little heavy. I knew Peanut was feeling better, but I still wanted him to see Dr. Charlie. At 9:00 a.m., I went to Jasmine's home with Peanut, she was running late from dropping her children off at their school. I went down the street, got a coffee, and turned into Jasmine's driveway when I saw her car. As soon as I pulled in, Jasmine came out of her house. "Oh thank God, you are here. My heart was breaking when I did not see you when I returned home. I was afraid he may have died last night."

While carrying Peanut's crate into her car, I said, "It was touch and go for a while but prayers were answered. His breathing has been better since 4:00 a.m."

Then I said, "Jasmine, you need to name this puppy. I was calling him Little Peanut, it's a weak name and this poor pup is weak. Pick out a strong name that will help him."

Right away she said, "Call him Lucky! He is Lucky he has you and so many people to care for him."

My face lit up, "Lucky! That's a perfect L name for this guy." It also made me feel a little bit better. I had been emotionally beating myself up over the fact that he was sick.

Jasmine drove off with Lucky! I went home, regardless of all the coffee I drank, I was exhausted. I checked on Lucy and the pups. Woke Chimayo up, made him go outside to the bathroom and eat his breakfast. I could feel my body was going to crash and I did not want

Chimayo to disturb me once it did. As soon as I reached my bed, I was asleep for close to seven hours.

Where's my son?

When I got up, I went into the garage to check on Lucy. Logan and Hunter were getting along great. Hunter was being very kind to Logan and this made him happy. Logan finally had a playmate. Lucy was very sad, staring at me with her head down. She was more than sad, she was depressed and angry at the same time. She did not understand why I would take one of her puppies away, again. I am sure her abused mind was racing with all the horrible things I could have done to him. "It's okay Lucy, I will be bringing your son back to you. You'll see him again, I promise."

I wish she understood because regardless of how gentle and calm my voice was, she stayed in the same depressed position longing for her third pup. I admired what a good mom she was.

Jasmine called me throughout the day to give me updates on Lucky. She had made videos of him dancing around. Clearly, he was feeling better. They were having so much fun with him that they were going to bring Lucky home with them later that evening.

When I picked Lucky up at Jasmine's home, it was explained that he went into a little breathing tank for his lungs. He had to stay in there for a couple hours, but they could see he was improving quickly. I was so relieved. All the thoughts I had about not being the right person to care for Lucky disappeared. I was so fortunate to have support from my neighbors. I sincerely believe it was divinely orchestrated for my mother to move next door to a veterinarian. They have generously helped my foster dogs countless times.

I was advised by Dr. Charlie that Lucky needed to be kept separate from his siblings for at least three more days. He was afraid he may get hurt roughhousing. I also had to watch him around Lucy. She could try to hide him from me again thinking she was protecting him. I promised to follow every instruction and be far more vigilant than I had been after dropping the poor pup on his head. Dr. Charlie and Jasmine kept telling me accidents happen, trying to make light of it, but it was hard for me to get over. I really scared Lucy, just when she was beginning to feel safe.

Let's get Better Together

When I left Dr. Charlie's I brought Lucky over to see my mom. She was sick too, I could think of nothing better than cuddling a puppy to cheer her up. My mother loves dogs as much as I do. She was lying on the sofa in her pajamas when I arrived. She sat up and I placed Lucky in her arms. He was exhausted from his day at the doctor's and playing with Jasmine's daughter. He allowed her to hold him on his back like a real baby and fell asleep in her arms. For the remainder of the week, Lucky would go to my mom's house during the day and returned to me at night.

The weather had warmed up, so Lucy and the pups wanted to go back into the garage. It was much bigger for them to run around in and easier for me to clean. I moved Lucky into my spare bathroom where he slept in his small crate filled with a cushiony bed and toys Jasmine had given him. He really enjoyed having his own room and toys. He also loved the extra attention he was getting as he recovered from pneumonia.

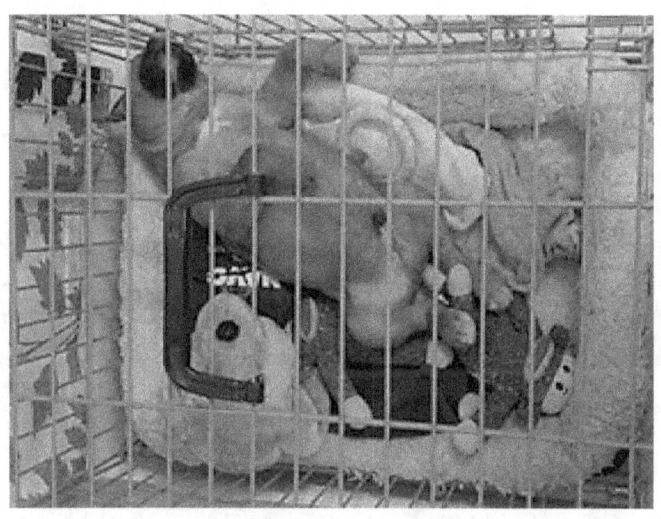

Lucky getting better in his own room

Mocho-Man in Back

As soon as Dr. Charlie said Lucky was able to see his family, I put him in the garage. Lucy was overjoyed to see him. She picked him up and carried him into the pool to smell all his new scents. Lucky was excited to see his brothers. He wagged his tail so fast I thought it may fly off. He jumped out of the pool and started running through the garage. Watching them in action, I understood why Lucky needed to be separated from them for so long. I regret not letting Lucy see him, but I was afraid she would hide him on me again.

Over the next 10 days, Lucky was healthy enough to go outside with them. He had gained weight and was now the same size as Hunter, and he wanted to be in charge again, too. His yappy *do not mess with me* bark returned. He initiated picking on Logan again, which Hunter sadly agreed too. When this occurred, Lucky had to stop playing with the other dogs. I would put him in his crate or I held him so the other pups could play in peace.

Lucky loved having his very own crate. This was his crate and he was not going to share it. I learned this when I placed all the pups in his crate to take them to the spay and neuter clinic. My mom came with me for the ride. This drive was much easier than when I took Lucy for her spay. As we were driving we would sporadically here loud sharp yaps coming from the crate. My mother looked in the back seat and saw that Lucky was fighting with his brothers to get them out of *his* crate. He clearly did not want them there. I pulled over to the side of the road and took Lucky out. Now he really felt special because my mom held him in her arms and he was able to look out the front window. This fascinated him and the rest the drive was quiet.

At the end of the day, I picked up the three boys. Logan and Hunter were medicated and confused as to why they were feeling so strange. I put them in the back of my car and they both went right to sleep. I decided not to put them in Lucky's crate.

Lucky felt fine as if nothing had happened. He marched around the back of the car and would make his harsh yapping sounds if he wanted one of his brothers to move. They were trying to rest but would get up, move a couple inches and fall back to sleep. Lucky continued to march around the back seat like a little soldier, yapping commands as he saw fit.

When we got home I took Lucky out of the car first and gave him to Lucy. When I took the pups from her in the morning, she was concerned. I heard her crying for them through the door, it was so sad. I promised her I would bring them back. When they returned she was ecstatic to see them. This time I thought her tail might fall off from wagging it so hard.

By now, they were close to 10 weeks old. They were more independent, and Lucy appreciated an occasional break from them. She was beginning to trust that when I took them I would bring them back. I knew the time was approaching for them to find loving forever homes. I wanted to make the transition as smooth as possible for her.

Sit-Stay-Hide

By this point, Lucky was 100% healthy. I started to train all three of the pups. They were very smart and treat oriented. I would stand in front of them with small treats and say "Sit."

Logan and Hunter would instantly sit, and both would get treats. Lucky did not want to sit or go into a down. He wanted nothing to do with any training commands. As soon I as started with the commands, he would walk away and find something better to do. But then, the little rascal would try to get the treat his brothers earned. He pulled Logan by the ear in jealousy. Even worse, he grabbed Hunter by the tail, and attempted to pull him through the yard to steal his treats. I was in shock at how quickly it would happen, and too flabbergasted to yell, "No!" in a timely manner.

Hunter and Logan enjoyed training commands so much that they would knock Dr. Charlie's pups and Faith out of the way in hopes of the treat. As soon as they heard the word *sit* they would run to the person and sit directly in front of them smiling. This prevented that person's own dog from getting the treat. I was thankful my pups were cute and had great smiles. They would have annoyed people otherwise. I am sure at times they probably did.

One evening I was trying to train the pups inside my house. Lucy would get the treats freely. I did not want to stress her out. As all three pups were agreeing to sit, I saw Lucy hiding on the other side of my kitchen wall peering in. She was doing all of the commands I requested but at a distance just to be safe. I was excited; progress was progress no matter how slow. With Lucy I needed to take inch worm steps, baby steps were too scary. Yet, every day I loved watching Lucy smile, wag her tail, be silly in the yard and gain confidence.

Lucky gets Lucky

Within 10 days of the pups being fixed Logan and Hunter had found their forever homes. Lucky was still waiting. There were plenty of applications for him, but the rescue was waiting for the ideal home. I realized Lucky found his perfect home when I placed his sick little body in my mother's arms. She had fallen in love with him while they would lie on the sofa together recovering from their illnesses. The days that Lucky was supposed to go to adoption events she protested that he was too young and little to attend. I reminded her that the other two pups had homes and pups smaller than Lucky would be at the event.

I told my mother I was leaving Lucky with her for a couple of days for her to decide if she wanted to adopt him. The first day she had him my uncle was visiting. In the evening I went over to see how things were going. My uncle said, "This is one great dog. He is so quiet. When he was done playing in the yard, he came in and went to sleep in the extra crate. We were worried because we couldn't find him and there he was sleeping soundly like a good boy."

My mother had started to train him. Lucky responded to her training because he liked being the center of attention. By the end of the week, my mother had decided that Lucky should be named Buddy Boy because they were best buds. Buddy knew he had his forever home when I would bring Logan over to visit him, it looked as if he was giving Logan a tour of his new house and new dog bed. Buddy even demonstrated what he looked like sleeping in his bed, but he did not want Logan to try any of his things.

I see Buddy almost every day. I wish he was still named Lucky to keep the L-name theme I started, but when a person fosters, they cannot pick out their forever name. At the end of the day, what is important is Buddy is happy and considered to be a member of the family.

Lessons Learned

It takes a village

In fostering Buddy, I learned the importance of community. I realized it takes a village to save these dogs. I also acknowledge that there are no small roles or parts in animal rescue. The mission to rescue Lucy and her pups started with one person taking a picture, another making a social media post, and then a team of volunteers in the Everglades of Florida committed to getting as many dogs out of the Redlands as possible.

Once Buddy and his family were caught, a volunteer in Tampa, FL., selflessly offered to drive directly to and from Miami, a minimum of 9 hours to bring four dogs to a safe home.

All the volunteers generously shared crates, beds, blankets, the swimming pool, and heaters to keep them cozy and warm. The monetary donations paid for medical and food. Plus, Dr. Charlie and Jasmine generously opening their clinic save to Buddy from dying, left me speechless.

I learned that every person who interacted with Buddy, his brothers, and mom played a significant role in bringing them to my home, keeping them healthy and fed.

Chapter 11
Hunter

Lucy's middle son was named Hunter. I refer to him as the follower or the pleaser. He was the fastest to learn all the training commands. He was also the first to be potty trained and caught on to anything I showed him quickly. Hunter looked just like Peanut only with thicker fur. As he grew, his snout was a little longer, like his mother's.

Peanut was the first puppy to learn how to give kisses. I held Peanut in my arms and Hunter watched a few times while I said, "Peanut kiss." Peanut would lean in and peck my cheeks or actual lips. I placed Peanut down and placed Hunter in my arms and on the first try he started giving kisses. This puppy lived to please and receive praise.

I did not name him Hunter, a neighbor who fell in love with him within the first few days of meeting him did. I believe it was Hunter's docile personality that was so appealing when he was alone with people. This puppy loved his mother. He was the crybaby on the ride home. He pulled himself out of the basket to yelp for her to get him. If Lucy came in from the yard to rest, Hunter was the first to follow, doing his best to be as close to her as he possibly could.

I know they say mothers do not have favorites but if Lucy did it was Hunter. Hunter was the only puppy that stayed with her every single night except when she was spayed. Peanut had to be separated and would visit her because of his illness. Logan spent a great deal of time with me when his siblings would pick on him. Lucy's consistent puppy was sweet Hunter. I believe Hunter comforted Lucy in times of confusion and stress, while she was learning to trust me or observe me doing things that did not make sense to her.

Hunter & Mommy

Hunter loved praise and being told, "Good boy," or "Good job."

His entire face would light up when he achieved something on his own, or figured out a training command. To this day, Hunter has one of the sweetest dog smiles I have ever seen. Friends would mention the pure joy in his eyes when he accomplished something or was accepting a well-earned compliment.

A Home for Hunter

Hunter's pictures were not posted on the adoption page because my neighbors had completed the adoption forms for him the first week he arrived. Unfortunately, they backed out. Their adult son found a dog that looked just like Hunter at a high kill shelter. This broke their heart and they adopted the older dog at the pound the exact same day they learned about him.

They understood that my rescue was very protective of the dogs in our care. We conduct background checks, reference checks, and home visits to ensure the dogs have a great life. They were confident that Hunter was going to find an ideal home, even if it was not with them. I knew that as well and I was happy they were able to save a dog from being euthanized.

I notified the rescue that Hunter was going to need a new home and a local photographer volunteered to take pictures of him and Peanut for their adoption page (this was before my mom decided to adopt Peanut).

Hunter got dressed up in a bandana for one picture and a bowtie in another. Pictures were taken outside of him running around, playing with his mother and being silly. Within 48 hours of the pictures being taken, adoption applications started coming in to meet Hunter.

Dogs- Feel, Love & Have Souls

A family that had adopted from the rescue previously was selected to be Hunters loving forever home. I was given the family's phone number and instantly called. A lady picked up the phone, her name was Darcy. We spoke about Hunter for close to 45 minutes or more. She and her husband owned a ranch, and they had dedicated their lives to working with rescued animals. Every animal at the ranch was rescued.

Darcy explained how she pulled three dogs from a high kill shelter and raised them together for seven years. Sadly, two of the three dogs passed away in the same month. Darcy went close to broke trying to help their beloved pets, but nothing they tried helped. The vets could not figure out what was the matter with her two dogs. Within seven days of each other, both dogs went to heaven. The remaining dog named Walter was completely healthy, but after losing his siblings he had gone into a deep depression.

Many argue that people give their dogs personalities, but they are wrong. It has been proven time and time again that animals, especially dogs DO have emotions, feelings, and high levels of intelligence. It has also been proven that dogs watch humans and have learned to mimic their facial expressions of smiling and laughing. They are able to learn this within days of being exposed to a positive loving person and environment. When people see pictures of my own dogs, I am often told that they look happy. They are actually happy, very happy, and to be honest they know they are spoiled too.

Therefore, when Darcy told me her poor dog Walter was depressed I completely understood. I have seen my dogs mourn the loss of their animal friends and their human family.

I explained to Darcy that Hunter was scheduled for his neuter and if all went well, he would be in his new home within a week. I asked her if she had picked out a new name for him. I would start calling him that name now, so he knew it when he arrived. His new name was to be Bear.

Is this Bearable?

The pups' neuter went very smoothly, besides Peanut commanding the pups where they could sleep on the ride home, there were no complications. About 48 hours after the surgery Darcy called, excited to get to meet her puppy. I knew this day was coming but it was harder than I imagined. Roger was visiting me. We had coffee on the porch while we watched the puppies play.

Lucy knew this was her last day with her son. For weeks the pups were wearing collars. Lucy chewed Bear's collar off his neck. We sat and watched her pick Bear up from playing with the other pups and take him to a separate part of the yard to cuddle him. She had her son nuzzled into her chest as closely as she could. "She knows he's leaving today," I told Roger.

"Oh, she definitely knows," he responded.

Then my silly mind went crazy, concerned that Bear may not be going to a good home. I knew I needed to shut my mind off. I picked up the phone asked Darcy if it would be okay if I drove Bear to her home. She was surprised because it was a two- hour drive, but appreciated not having to drive mid-way to get him herself. I explained that I knew Bear was going to an amazing home, but giving him up, even though he is not my puppy, was hard for me. After all, I had cared for this puppy and his mother for 10 weeks. I watched him grow and shared in many of his first-time experiences. It was impossible not to fall in love. I needed to see where Bear was going for myself. This would help me to let go.

Darcy agreed and gave me the directions to her home. After Roger left, I went through the pictures I had taken of Bear so his new family could see how big he got and how he cared for his mother. They were adopting a very considerate and sensitive puppy. I left Lucy and Bear alone until it was time to go. Logan and Peanut were placed in their play area in the garage. One on one, Peanut was nice to Logan.

I used Peanut's crate for the drive. Peanut loved his crate so much that Bear being allowed to be the only puppy in it was very special. Bear stretched out on his back and slept with all four feet in the air the entire ride. When I got to the house, I took Bear out of the crate. I held him close to my chest and whispered in his ear, "I love you, when I place you on the ground you are going to start your new amazing life. Do not be afraid, these people already love you." With a long hug and a couple of kisses on Bear's forehead, I turned around and placed him into Darcy's loving arms - his new mom.

I sincerely thought I was going to cry and be depressed for a couple of days after doing this, but I was wrong. Darcy and her husband were so kind, I smiled the whole ride home. Darcy instantly cuddled Bear, as she held him she gave me a brief story about all of the horses and dogs she rescued over the years. They had a lot of land for Bear to run on, more than what he had with me. As we were talking, Darcy's husband Toby came out of the house, from the porch he yelled, "Invite her in, Walter wants to meet his new brother."

Darcy handed Bear to me and allowed me to carry him into his new home. Toby smiled at me and gestured with his hand for us to walk into the house. As I entered the living room, there was a black lab mix stretched out on their sofa. This dog was lifeless, he had one of the saddest expressions on his face I have ever seen on a dog, and I have seen far too many sad dogs. This had to be Walter. He did not look up when he heard us. He remained in the same pitiful position on the sofa, taking a few deep sighs. I looked at Toby, without saying anything he nodded his head as if to say, *I know, this is one miserable dog.* In a cheerful voice, Toby said, "Walter, look you have a new brother! This little guy is for you!"

Walter quickly turned around and looked up, he knew the word brother. I smiled and placed Bear on the floor. The two dogs wagged tails and touched noses. Walter looked up at me with a smile as kind as Bears. As Bear and Walter kissed and wagged their tails at each other, we could see Walter's body language improve. The depression was being lifted away. As Walter and Bear got acquainted, Darcy and I went into the other room to complete the adoption forms. She generously gave me a tour of her home to ease my mind while explaining the wonderful life Bear was going to have. I sat at the kitchen table with Darcy while she filled out the final adoption paperwork, gazing into the living room to watch Bear and Walter become friends. Walter would run into the kitchen with a twinkle in his eye and smile at me. If he could talk, I believe he was thanking me for bringing him Bear. The playful difference in Walter's mannerism within five minutes of meeting Bear was remarkable. Walter really missed having other dogs around. Bear was his surprise blessing.

As I was about to leave, Bear ran to me to go home with me. I got down on my knees, picked him up, and gave him another big hug. I grabbed two dog treats from my bag and gave them to Darcy to hold. I whispered in his ear "I love you - this is your new home and your new brother. You are going to be very happy here, I promise."

I placed Bear in Darcy's arms with the treats to give him and Walter and quickly exited the house. Toby walked me to my car. I felt amazing about leaving Bear in such a wonderful home. Toby thanked me for fostering Lucy and caring for Bear for 10 weeks. He said, "I know people underestimate what fosters and rescues do, but your fostering this pup has made a grand difference our life. Walter is happy again and we have loved Bear from the moment we set eyes on him. Drive safely, we will keep in touch."

Darcy and Toby kept in touch for about three months. Walter was so happy that he had a new brother, and he successfully came out of his depression. Bear sleeps in Darcy's arms every night. I learned that he snores very loudly. He likes to look at the horses from a distance, and every day is getting a little bit braver around them. Darcy, Toby, Walter, Bear, and the horses are very happy together.

When I returned home without Bear, Lucy did not seem too concerned. Possibly because Logan and Peanut had driven her nuts or she was suppressing her emotions. I did not mention his name in case it would cause her to be sad. I continued the same care for her as I had over the past couple of months. Peanut seemed the most concerned about Bear leaving. When Logan, Lucy and I would practice training commands, Peanut suddenly became very compliant. Bear's leaving made this young puppy acknowledge that his time with me was short. Peanut was very happy living with me and started to be very obedient in order to stay. I make jokes that since Jasmine changed his name to Lucky his wish came true, getting a wonderful forever home, down the street from me.

Lesson Learned

The lesson I learned through Bear's adoption was to be open to others' kind-hearted nature. There are amazing people in this world, truly amazing! There are people who can care for and love animals better than I can. This recognition felt as if a huge weight had been lifted off my shoulders. I became more confident that I was going to be able to help more dogs find homes as wonderful as Bears'. The whole experience still brings a smile to my face.

Chapter 12
Logan

As much as I tried to fight it, this little guy stole my heart. Logan was a loner, whether he wanted to be or not. As a researcher and writer, I tend to see myself as an introverted loner as well. Maybe this is why I clicked so well with this little pup.

As I already explained, he was picked on when he first arrived. Mother dogs and cats can have a litter, and not all puppies have the same father. In the beginning, I wondered if Logan was even Lucy's real pup, but she cuddled him, nursed him and was just as protective of him as the other pups. It did not matter who his real mother was, he was loved. A few weeks later I did realize that Logan was Lucy's because all three puppies developed the same facial expressions and mannerisms (body language).

Within 24 hours of the pups coming into my home, Logan was constantly in my arms. I would hear barking in the garage, and I would go in to see what was going on. There was scared little Logan with his head hidden in a blanket or in the corner, and the other two pups were simultaneously barking at him. I would hurry in, snatch him up and until it was time for him to eat, I would do everything one-handed. As soon as I would return him to Lucy, she would lift her head, and he would nuzzle into her to take a nap.

The other puppies were not mean, this is how animals behave. I would sit on the floor, play with the pups, and try to get Lucy comfortable with me being around me. Out of the blue, Logan's brothers would decide they wanted to pick on him.

One day I came home from a meeting, and Logan had broken out of the playpen I had kept all of them in. Frantically, I looked through the garage calling his name. I could not get a response from him. This led my mind to race to worst case scenario with Logan, until I found him frozen behind my clothes dryer. I gently encouraged him to come to me, but he would not move, he was literally scared stiff. After a few attempts of trying to reach to pick him up from under that dryer, I had to squeeze between my washer and dryer and pick him up. He was motionless, even in my arms. I brought him into the house and gave him some puppy treats to try and cheer him up. It took a few treats, but he came around.

A few days later I was with my friend who was also fostering a litter of pups. She explained that the pup that looked a little different ended up at the vet from being picked on so much. After finding this out, Logan was with me about 65 % of the time. Until Peanut got sick, Logan came with me everywhere. Of course, this created an even stronger bond between us than I wanted.

I discussed with a few people about keeping Logan, and no one thought it was a good idea. My reputation was with senior dogs. Publically, I had made a commitment to help senior dogs that are harder to adopt. Now I was going to adopt a puppy! Let's be honest Logan was a super cute puppy too. A week after the pups arrived at my house I was sent a couple of doggie outfits. Peanut and Hunter were too small to for them to properly fit, but the plaid shirt fit Logan perfectly. Logan sat on my lap as I put it on, "All set." I said and put him down so he could run around.

Logan thought the shirt was fantastic. He was so happy that he started posing and dancing around. He proudly showed his mother the shirt, and was too excited to acknowledge her confused look. I sat on the garage floor mesmerized by Logan's joy. The way he pranced and ran to get the shirt on, this was the exact same way Luke would run up to me to put his shirt on. Love from Luke 1, explains why the vet had recommended shaving Luke and why he needed to wear a t-shirt.

I placed Logan on a red dish towel, wearing his red and white plaid shirt, and took a few really cute photos. I then put a plaid bandana on Hunter and a blue bow-tie on Peanut for adoption pics. I sent them to the rescue and put them on my social media sites. They were a hit! Logan in his plaid shirt began to get a great deal of inquiries for adoption. This was good news. Logan, and all the pups deserved loving forever homes and the fact that people wanted to learn more about them so quickly was promising. But my heart sank knowing I was going to have to give Logan up.

When Peanut was well enough to return to Lucy and his brothers, I had to start removing Logan from the group again. When it was Hunter and Logan, they got along great. Logan was delighted to have another pup to play with him. Hunter enjoyed teaching Logan all the games he had missed out on. Sadly, within hours of Peanuts return, they started to gang up and bark at Logan again.

By now Logan had two sets of required puppy shots, so he started to come in the car and run errands with me. I would take him to my mom's house to play with Faith. Dr. Charlie had two puppies going through a training course. The trainers would use Logan as a distraction while trying to have his puppies obey commands. Logan loved when he got to be the distraction. I loved that Faith was so kind to him and he enjoyed observing the training classes.

Many neighbors started to call Logan by the name Luke. I would quickly turn my head and say, "No, that's Logan, not my Luke."

I was not offended by the comments, but I did not want Luke to be forgotten. It had only been five months since Luke had passed away. I was working on my book about him, and the pain was still fresh.

Logan gets a Home

One of my closest friends, Roger, was briefly transferred to my area for work. He started staying with me close to every other week while I had the pups. He fell in love with Logan as much as I did and wanted to adopt him. I have known him and his family for over 20 years; I have celebrated many holidays with them and have seen them go above and beyond for the dogs they rescue. Roger went home from his business trip to tell his parents and brother about Logan. If they agreed to help him, he was going to fill out the adoption forms and give Logan the most amazing home a dog could have.

Roger adopting Logan felt right. I would be able to see him and watch him grow up while continuing to help other dogs. Once Roger got home he called me and said his family wanted to meet Logan, but they had one concern. They feared their senior dog would feel he was being replaced. I explained that I would talk to the rescue, get care for Lucy and the pups, drive to their home and introduce Logan to their senior dog.

Luke, is that you?

Roger's company kept sending him to Tampa. He was able to spend a great deal of time with the pups, learn their personality and help me with Lucy. Chimayo loves Roger and was overjoyed at the amount of time he got to spend with him. Every time Roger's company sent him to Tampa, Logan's trip to West Palm Beach got delayed.

One day Logan and I went to my mom's house after running a bunch of errands. She asked me what was going on with Logan's adoption. I explained that if Roger was not going to take Logan, I was going to adopt him. I fell in love with Logan, and I wanted to him to be my dog. Logan quietly sat in the room but was listening to the entire conversation. He understood what was being said too.

When I got home from my mothers, I let everyone outside to play in the yard. Logan did not want play with his brothers at all. Outside, all the pups played nicely with Lucy. Inside was when they would get into mischief and pick on Logan. He went out to the bathroom, quickly came back in, and followed me everywhere I went, my four-legged furry shadow.

I was in my guest bedroom hanging a picture on the wall. Quietly, Logan came behind me and kissed the back of my right knee. I froze I'm not sure how long I stood still holding the picture facing the wall, finally I turned around, got on my knees and looked at Logan. He sat down in front of me, smiling while looking up toward me, for a reaction. "Luke, is that you?" I asked wide-eyed and in complete amazement.

Logan sat looking back at me with a smile on his face. I sat on the floor, crossed my legs and placed him on my lap. He nuzzled in, and I started petting him. "Was that a sign that you want to stay with me? Did an angel tell you to kiss my knee?" I asked.

For over 22 years, I have been active in animal rescue, Luke was the only dog who would randomly come up behind me and give me a kiss behind my right knee. I always thought it was odd, but did not realize how different it was until Logan did the exact same thing. It was too much of a coincidence. This confirmed Logan wanted to be my dog.

"I am filling out the adoption forms tonight," I told him. "You're officially Logan Sweeney, and this is your forever home."

Logan and I sat together until his brothers came running in the house, and joined us in the spare bedroom. All three pups played nicely together, and on their own ran into the garage for bed.

Once Chimayo was in bed after his short and sweet evening routine, I went to the rescue's adoption webpage and filled out the application to for Logan. Within a few hours, I received an email back saying, "What a lucky puppy Logan is, congratulations, foster fail!"

I felt very calm and pleased with my decision to keep Logan. I worried about his adoption more than the other pups. Maybe foster mom's intuition, but I am fortunate Logan was the puppy I did adopt.

The next morning I opened the garage door for the pups and Lucy to run through the house to the backyard. Logan knew he was mine. As soon as he saw me, he stopped running with his brothers and ran to me. He stretched out on his back and waited for his tummy to be rubbed. From that day forward Logan was my little shadow. If I went outside he came with me, he would play with the other pups, but preferred to be with me. Regardless of what pups name I would call, Logan would run as fast as he could into my arms.

As time progressed even more of Logan's mannerisms mimicked Luke's. Logan sleeps in the exact same spot in the house that Luke used to. If he feels I did not spend enough time with him, he cries similar to the way Luke would howl to get my attention. He lays across my lap the same way too. My friend, who cried the first time she visited after Luke passed away agreed Logan made it feel as if Luke never left. She said, "He acts the same as Luke did only in a different body."

Many of my friends laughed at me when I finally admitted Logan acts like Luke, they said, "Yes, he has reminded me of Luke from day one, the way he walks, smiles, just everything about that puppy makes him a Luke mini-me, a surprise gift from God just for you!"

I am happy I adopted Logan, as the story continues I learned exactly why Logan was meant to be my dog. The fact that he acts so much like Luke is an additional blessing, motivating me to keep the promise I made, to always help animals in need.

Chapter 13
Really Logan-Really!

Once Hunter and Peanut were adopted Logan came everywhere dogs were welcomed. I noticed that Logan loved all dogs, and wanted to make friends with them. He would initiate play, but when he got close to the other dog, they would snap, and try to bite him. They were not friendly to him at all. They wanted nothing to do with him. I was so confused by this. I shared with my friends that I felt like my dog was always getting bullied. I was scared he was going to become mean and resentful of other dogs if he got attacked. My poor Chimayo never emotionally recovered from the other dog beating him up.

One day when Logan and I were out running errands. My car was stopped at a stop sign. Logan had his head out the window, and a man rode his bike past us. This was something new to Logan, he never saw anyone ride a bike. He leaned forward to get a closer look.

While watching him from my rear view mirror, I realized I forgot to put the safety latch on the window. Logan fell out of the window head first into the parking lot. I just saw his two furry brown legs flip out of my car. I put my car in park and started rambling to myself in a panicky voice, *my puppy fell out the window, my puppy fell out of my window!*

I ran to the side of the car, little Logan was standing there, looking shocked and scared. I picked him up, and let him sit on my lap the whole ride home. I was so mad at myself, how could I be so careless and stupid, forgetting to lock the puppy window. I wanted to scream in frustration, but I did not want to scare Logan, he was sleeping on my lap.

When I got home, I placed him in his crate to sleep. I watched him carefully for 24 hours, and he seemed fine. I was relieved, until a week later when he started to limp and favor his front left leg. I made an appointment to see Dr. Charlie. Embarrassed I explained how Logan fell out of my car window. This was as shameful as dropping Peanut on his head. I was so discouraged and ashamed of myself until he said, "One of our puppies fell out of the window too. They are so fast, accidents happen!"

We both had a good laugh. Dr. Charlie took Logan in the back to x-ray his front paws. When it was over he brought Logan back into the room, Logan was about 35 pounds now, but thought he was much smaller he climbed on my lap, stretched out on his back and started to snore while waiting for the results. When Dr. Charlie came into the room, he had a sad look on his face. I was confused, "What is it?" I said. I expected him to tell me Logan had broken his paw or leg.

Dr. Charlie responded, "It's a good thing Logan fell out of the window so we could take these x-rays. From reviewing Logan's x-rays, he has a rare bone disease called panosteitis, a bone disease characterized by bones shedding and possibly breaking very easily."

As Dr. Charlie was talking, I started to hug my snoring puppy tighter. I was told that Logan could grow out of the disease, within 18 months, if I stunted his growth. This required putting him on a low protein adult dog food, 22% or lower. He needed food and vitamins high in omega 3 and glucosamine. I also needed to be vigilant with his play. Logan, could very easily shatter a bone while prancing around.

I know I had a sad look on my face. I wanted a healthy dog to have fun with. I had been through so much with Luke and Chimayo was a senior, I was devastated to learn my very special puppy was sick. This explained why other dogs tried to hurt Logan when he wanted to play with them. They could smell that he was not healthy and did not want him to be around them.

I paid the vet bill and drove home with Logan in silence. Logan was enjoying looking out the window without a I care in the world. He was clueless about the news Dr. Charlie gave me. When we got home, I left Logan in the car, ran into my house and got the unopened bag of dog food I recently purchased. We went to the pet store to exchange it for a low protein adult food. I explained to the cashier Logan needed adult pet food with no more than 22% protein. The cashier helped me flip over almost all the bags of food to read the ingredients. Once the new food was selected, I got him some vitamins and ran into the supermarket to get additional supplements to add to his food.

Why Me! Why NOT Me!

Logan had a great day. When we got home he played with his mother then they both had a nice snooze together. He enjoyed his new vitamins and food. The bad news about being sick with a rare disease did not bother him one bit. I was the one taking it hard. I went into the other room to lie down and hug Chimayo. We cuddled together, and I watched some feel-good movies to lift my depressed mood. Nothing helped; I was full of self-pity about my sick puppy.

I woke up the next morning to feeling worse than the day before. My friend was having a pool party to celebrate his birthday, but I felt too gloomy to attend. I fed my dogs, made my coffee and sat on my patio watching them play. Lucy was very gentle with Logan, so I had nothing to worry about.

I sat on my porch in a miserable mood, watching my two rescued dogs play without a care in the world. While they were having fun, I kept thinking to myself, *Why me - this is so unfair, another sick dog! I wanted a healthy normal dog! Why are you doing this to me, God? Is a healthy puppy really too much to ask for?*

While mumbling complaints about how horrible I felt my life was, it was suddenly made clear why Logan was meant to be my dog. I had experience with sick dogs, I watched Luke defy every odd and health issue placed against him. Luke is in veterinarian research books for being the oldest husky to receive treatment and have a remarkable recovery. He was given 6 months to live, yet lasted 18 months -18 fun-loving months! With faith, Logan would recover and have as much fun, if not more than Luke had. Who better to have a dog with a rare disease than me?

If Luke was able to be healed than Logan could be too. Logan could have easily broken his bones when he fell out the window but didn't. I needed to recognize we were already receiving divine miracles and blessings. It was my attitude toward caring for Logan that needed to change. Once I had this realization, I went onto my social media page to share what the vet had explained to me and requested prayers for Logan.

Social Media Post June 28, 2016

On Friday Logan was diagnosed with panosteitis, a bone disease characterized by bones shedding and possibly breaking very easily. Only 3% of dogs have this. Although, I am sad Logan has this disease. It is curable, I am 100% confident Logan will be strong and healthy. I feel hand-picked by God to be given this dog. I have an abundance of experience working with special needs animals. Who better for Logan to belong to!

Once I made this post, I called my dogs in from the yard and got myself ready for the pool party. I was the last one to arrive, but everyone was happy to see me. I explained that I was depressed about the news I got about Logan. One friend instantly said, "Well he's lucky he has you, who better to have this dog, he'll be fine! This is right up your alley."

A few friends from my animal rescue community commented, with similar positive posts, agreeing that if anyone could handle a puppy with a rare disease, it was me.

Don't Mess with Logan

It took a couple months to get Logan on a good diet that would most effectively help him. While caring for Logan, he became a bit spoiled. In fact, sometimes he was a spoiled brat. I learned in the first couple months that Logan was very smart, had a good memory, and wow-he could hold a grudge!

One time I had a former co-worker Amber, came to my home because she needed help with some paperwork. She had been to my home plenty of times before, she was fine around Luke and Chimayo, but for some reason, she was not fond of Logan. As we were in my office that was now partially converted to Logan and Lucy's room, she seemed irritated if he came over to her for attention. To prevent further distractions I put Logan in his crate in the room with us while we reviewed the paperwork. When we were almost done, Logan started to bark at us. He was about four months old, and he wanted to get out of his crate to play. Suddenly, Amber jumped out of my office chair and yelled he is going to bite to me. The chair had wheels on it, and she pushed it right into Logan's crate. I was too shocked to be angry. Logan froze in his crate looking up at her with wide eyes. Before I could say it, Amber said, "I better get going," and hurried out of my house.

When she left, I took Logan out of the crate, brought him to Lucy where he was drowned with affection. Logan was pleased about this but secretly was very angry that the chair was pushed at him. A few weeks later I took Logan with me to a party. My friend lives by the water, and some of the guests were kayaking. Logan and I walked onto the boat dock to say hi to everyone. Friends taking turns kayaking, were coming on and off of the pier. As I chatted, Logan sunbathed. All of a sudden, Logan jumped up to his feet and in a very defensive manner started sternly barking at a kayaker coming in. Then I heard a woman's voice shriek, "Oh no, he doesn't like me."

I got closer to Logan to see who he was barking at and it was Amber. We had to leave the dock, so she felt comfortable getting out of the kayak. I took Logan into the house there were plenty of people around to distract him from teasing Amber. Yet, Logan had two more experiences with Amber where he expressed his dislike for her. One day, my house was quiet, and I was working on my computer. All the sudden Logan started his stern voice barking and was jumping at the window. I went to the front of the house to see what was going on. It was Amber trying to drop off a few books. I did not get to talk to her because she dropped them at my door and quickly ran to her car.

Amber moved away, but the very last encounter Logan had with her was when a mutual friend invited her to my house for a pool party. At first, Logan ignored her. There were plenty of people telling him how great he was. I did not foresee any problem with them being together until the end of the party. There were about 15 pairs of shoes scattered around the pool, out of all the shoes, Logan specifically chose Amber's shoes to eat. I apologized to her and offered to buy or fix her shoes. She preferred to have them fixed. She was a good sport about it, even when people were laughing and saying, "Wow that dog really doesn't like you."

That was the last I saw of Amber, she moved away for a job opportunity. Logan moved onto teasing my mother. Logan likes to visit my mother's house for a short period of time. Buddy gets jealous when Logan visits his home for too long. Logan gets jealous if I take another dog for a walk in front of him. One day I took Buddy for a walk and told Logan I would be back quickly. When I walked out the door with Buddy, Logan went over to Buddy's bed, grabbed it with his teeth and threw it. This ripped Buddy's bed causing my mom to yell at him. He really did not like that. When I got back with Buddy, Logan and I went home. The next time we visited, while I was talking to my mom, Logan went into her bedroom. All of a sudden he ran out and went to the front door wanting to go home. Annoyed my mom looked at Logan and said to me, "Why did you even bother to bring him if he never wants to stay."

She got up, went into her bedroom and let out a yell. Logan put his ears back, and his eyes widened. I ran in to see what was wrong. Logan had gotten on her bed and ran around in circles until he pulled the comforter, sheets and mattress cover into a ball in the middle of her bed. I helped her make her bed while Logan silently waited to leave. I am sure he felt a little guilty, my mother complained about his bad behavior the entire time we fixed up her bed.

For the most part, Logan was great puppy. The majority of people love him, and he loves them back. His bone condition was not slowing him down but I still worried about Logan not liking other dogs because so many of them rejected him. I decided it was time to start fostering younger puppies, primarily for Logan to have friends.

Chapter 14

Luna

I contacted the rescue, and I explained Logan's medical condition. I told them I wanted to start fostering pups again, solely so Logan could have friends. Within 48 hours they had found the perfect furry friend for him.

***#Savethepups*!**

The rescue had pulled a purebred pregnant German Shepard from a kill shelter in Georgia. They had transported her to a foster home in Florida. The foster family called the mother dog Maci. Maci gave birth to ten purebred German Shepard puppies. They were magnificent!

There are many stories such as Maci's. I cannot accept the excuse from a person stating the needed to go to a breeder because they wanted a purebred dog with no issues. The sad reality is many breeders do it for the money. The dogs in most foster care programs are being provided with excellent medical treatment. They are given the required food and vitamins they need to ensure they are physically and emotionally healthy.

I have had breeders personally contact me to ask about how to care for the new puppies and mother dog. I take my time to explain the best food, supplements, and items needed to assist all the dogs. One lady got angry with me and said, "I feed them whatever is on sale. I can't afford to do these things for these dogs. You're ridiculous!"

The lady slammed the phone down in my ear. She had found me online. I sent her digital coupons and tips, to help her afford all her dogs, but I never heard back. It was clear that every dog that was in a foster home with the rescues I am active with received better care than the poor puppies the woman had bred. The sad reality is, many people breed their dogs because they need money, not because they care about the dogs or the puppies.

Strong & Shiny

When I first met Luna, I was asked to transport her and her litter of brothers and sisters to various other foster homes throughout Florida. Luna was the runt; she had a big grin on her face when I put her in my car. It was clear this tiny pup was fearless. Her siblings were concerned as to what was happening to them, and where they were being taken, but not her. She sat up straight in the back seat of the car, ready for whatever fun adventure was about to begin.

I was told by the rescue that this little one was born with an extra vertebra and may need to have back surgery. It was requested that I care for her because of my experience with special needs dogs.

Transporting Little Luna

I have to say transporting five, 8-week old pups was pretty easy. Once the puppies felt safe, they all became excited about the car ride and enjoyed trying to look above the car window to see the outside world. By the end of the day after playing with names in my mind, I asked the other fosters what they thought of naming my small girl Luna. Everyone instantly agreed it was a beautiful name for a good-looking dog.

Of course, because I believe the meaning of the name is important, I looked up the definition of Luna first. In some cultures, it was the moon, other variations of Luna meant strong and shiny. I felt with her back problems, she needed a name that symbolized she would strive regardless of any physical setbacks. Little did I know that the naming of this pup was going to become as meaningful as the name I had given Luke.

When Luna's last sibling was dropped off, she started to cry in the back seat of the car. My mother reached back, took her onto her lap and made silly sounds the entire way home. Luna responded with comical facial expressions.

When I brought Luna to my home it was clear she had the perfect name. From the time I placed her down on the floor, she became a fearless, sassy, firecracker! To introduce her to Lucy and Logan, I put them in the backyard. I then placed Luna down next me, on the screened-in patio floor. Lucy and Logan came up to the patio screen to look at her. She bravely sat next to me and barked at them.

Luna then confidently stood up to walk toward them. For the first time, I could see her back legs wobble and understood what the rescue was talking about. She reminded me of a newborn fawn or calf trying to stand up for the first time, shaking as they gradually made their way to a standing position. Luna had a lump on her back from the extra vertebra. The vet explained the vertebra prevented her brain from properly sending signals to her hind legs. I observed how she walked for a few days. She was able to get around and was clueless that she different, she was simply slower than the other dogs. I noticed that each time she woke up from a nap, she would walk differently from the time before. She was altering her movement to favor whatever part of her body was weak or sore. I decided on my own that I was going to start giving her the same vitamins as Logan. I saw how they were helping him. I knew they would not harm her, so she started on them the same week she arrived.

Once I realized Luna was not afraid of my dogs, and they were curious about her I brought everyone inside. Logan went crazy in excitement to have a new friend. Much like a young child, he did not want her to play with all of his toys. While Luna was exploring her new surroundings, she waddled over to the toy box. Logan instantly got up and ran over to the toy box as well. He grabbed three of his favorite toys, got up on the sofa and hid them behind the back cushion so Luna could not reach them. They were just for him. It was so funny, one of those moments that I wished I had my camera, but didn't.

Lucy, on the other hand, was not too thrilled to have Luna stay with us. Cheerfully, I said, "Lucy, look at our puppy!"

Intentionally, she turned her head in the other direction so she would not have to acknowledge Luna. After that first introduction,

Luna did not make it any easier for Lucy to like her. Lucy wanted to show Luna she was going to be the alpha dog. She would sit high on the sofa to show her dominance, looking down at Luna, giving her a low growl. Now, most puppies would know this is a sign to be cautious around the adult dog and shy away. Not feisty little Luna. She instantly mimicked every growling face shown to her, even if Lucy showed her all her teeth. Luna was delighted, wagging her tail, and would playfully bark at Lucy to make another mean face as if to say, *that was funny! Do it again!*

Although, it was cute to watch an 8 week old, 10-pound puppy do this, it really made Lucy mad. I had to keep Luna on a leash, by my side to ensure she would not antagonize Lucy too much. It got to the point that as soon as Luna would see Lucy, she would wag her tail show all her teeth and playfully growl. It was funny, but I could not have this firecracker puppy getting hurt, and Lucy deserved respect!

Regardless, of her physical differences, Luna was fearless around Lucy. In fact, she was courageous toward almost everything she encountered. A bug walking on the ground, a leaf blowing in the wind, you name it, she was on top of it and barking. My friends and I joked that I should have picked a name out that meant dull and boring versus strong and shiny.

One day we had a tropical storm. Logan and Luna went out to use the bathroom. A strong wind picked Luna up and tossed her into the pool. The water was like ocean waves, plus we had heavy rain. I ran outside and scooped her up out of the water. I wanted to cuddle her while I dried her off. I held her close to me, and she gently placed her head under my chin. It was a tender moment, I could feel my love and protectiveness for her pouring out of me, but that only lasted seconds. As soon as we got on the lanai, Luna started to wiggle and push away from me, she wanted to get down and play more. Being tossed in the pool scared me more than it had scared her.

Luna was brave, fun loving and extremely smart. Her first foster was able to train all 10 puppies to go outside to the bathroom within eight weeks. Within the first week of Luna living with me, she learned the same training commands as Logan. I will be boastful and admit Luna was potty trained and knew basic training commands by 9 weeks old! She never had an accident in my home.

I was so impressed that Luna knew her puppy commands I brought her to my mom's house to show her off. First was sit, then down and then stay. As Luna was in her sit-stay command, we were praising her for being such a good girl. Buddy, who knows all the commands, but refused to do them, made a worried face, and on his own, he did the exact same as Luna to receive praise as well. It was hysterical, one of those moments when you want to laugh, but have to be serious. It was hard to be encouraging, and keep a straight face. Buddy is very sensitive and would not have appreciated us laughing at him.

When Luna had to go to the bathroom, she would start to cry. This was great during the day, but at night she slept in the spare bathroom, in a little bed with a blanket and toys. She had to get up about twice a night. I was happy I heard her, but I was not happy that I had to wake up. However, Luke had trained me on how bad it could be, Luna's whimpering beforehand was better than cleaning up her bed and toys because I was a lazy foster dog mom. I would remind myself her midnight cries were temporary.

Sometimes Luna would get up to go to the bathroom, then she would want to play or have me stay to keep her company until she fell back to sleep. I understood that Luna was only 9 weeks old, everything happening to her since she left her siblings and mom was new, scary and, I am sure at times, lonely. Before coming to my house, she was sleeping with her brothers and sisters. Now she slept alone, I am sure she missed all of them dearly. I know it is hard for me to get sleep in a new place. For all these reasons, I would sit on the bathroom floor, lay Luna in her bed and put a blanket over her. I would pet her and read out loud until she fell asleep.

By the third week of Luna's stay, we were getting up about three times a night. Two times to go to the bathroom, and another time because she was hungry. Luna was going through a growth spurt and needed to eat more. Because of her extra vertebrae and difficulty walking at times, I wanted her to always be provided with the vitamins and nutrients necessary to keep her healthy. She responded quickly to the additional supplements I had placed her on.

The other thing about Luna was she appreciated being respected, and she always wanted to have a good time. If she felt disrespected by Logan or any other dog I would bring into the house she would let them know. When I would tell her that was enough, she would bark at me or try to nip my finger when I would come over and sternly say, "No!"

Luna could wear Logan out. One time she grabbed him by the ear when he sat on the floor with her. I quickly separated them, and Logan got up on the sofa away from her. She was too little to get up on the furniture by herself. He went behind the cushion grabbed one of the toys he had hidden and sat down to chew it. Luna looked up at him in shock that he had stopped playing with her. He looked back at her, his facial expression that said, *No more fun today, kid, you're mean!*

Luna tried to hoist herself up to get on the sofa too. When she realized she couldn't do it, she threw a loud barking puppy tantrum at him. As if to say, *Get back down here, I want to play more!*

To break up these disagreements I would pick Luna up, and allow her to whimper and vent her frustration while I petted her. Within five minutes she would relax on my lap. I would return to working on my computer.

Within four weeks Luna was able to run as fast as the other dogs. She no longer wobbled when she walked. A person would have to pay very close attention to notice a difference in how she walked next to another dog. Her back legs rarely gave out on her. She could stand herself up and lean against the sofa using her hind legs. I knew she was completely healthy. Two vets examined her and everyone agreed that if she was kept on the diet, I placed her on she was going to have a normal healthy life. I understood this meant she was ready to find her loving forever home.

Logan & Luna sharing a bed

Logan & Baby Luna Best Friends

The thought of giving Luna up did make me sad. I worried about other people losing their temper with Luna's sassy attitude. I had to remind myself about the great homes other dogs in foster care have gone too. She was extremely cute, many considered her beautiful and she was fun to watch. But she would sass anyone until she got what she wanted, or she got the barking and whining from the insult off her chest. Logan and his brother Buddy taught her the joys of digging holes in the backyard and one day the three of them chewed up Lucy's bed. When I came out and saw the mess, I scolded them. Tiny Luna tried to hide her face thinking I could not see her, but she quickly realized I could. So she playfully ran into the other room while I did my best to make everyone try to feel guilty for ruining their mother's bed. I wanted them to at least pretend they were sad for getting caught. I know Lucy was upset about her bed being ruined.

I knew that whoever adopted Luna would be informed again and again and AGAIN of the additional care and patience she required. They needed to have experience working with highly intelligent dogs so they would not lose their patience with her. The rescue I was volunteering with did extensive background checks on everyone. They conducted home visits, contacted the veterinarian, and ensured all other animals in the house were fixed, up to date on their shots, heartworm and flea medications.

Regardless of Luna's physical disability she was going to need to go through training. I had taught her the basics; sit, stay and come, but she was going to need a very intelligent owner that she would not outsmart.

I had Luna for one month. I provided her a supportive and loving environment that inspired her to thrive regardless of her humpback, strange walk and extra vertebra. Over that time I placed her on the same diet as Logan. She was given high levels of glucosamine chondroitin with msm (6 pills a day). Luna no longer dragged her back legs. She was in my pool at least twice a week for water therapy. I never allowed her to be seen as different or special needs by myself or anyone who encountered her. She was encouraged to run and play as if nothing was wrong. The rescue was sincerely pleased with the progress she made. Both vets agreed that if this care was kept up, she would never need to have back surgery. Luna only required swimming and daily vitamins to have a long, happy and healthy life.

Once it was determined Luna could be adopted it was clearly stated in the adoption forms of her needs. Copies of the x-rays and care requirements from two vets who specialize in spinal injuries were included with her adoption packet too.

The family that adopted Luna had to legally agree to keep her on her daily vitamins, take her for very short walks and allow her to swim at least twice a week if not more in their pool. Trust me, watching Luna thrive made me fall in love with her. I was going to make it extremely clear that nothing should prevent Luna from having a great life. Luna was a beautiful, bright, and very healthy puppy I knew a lot of people wanted to adopt her.

On September 18, 2016, Luna got adopted by a family who had previously rescued an adult German Shepard. The family made him a part of the family and treated him very well. The man made himself appear as if he loved Luna and would continue to provide a loving environment for her. I was sad to see her leave, but understood there were more dogs in need of a foster, and I wanted Logan to have as many friends as possible.

Adopting a Pure Bred

As I have briefly explained, many people have shared their concerns with me about adopting a dog versus going to a breeder. Dixie, Luke, and Luna are a few of the purebred dogs I have had in my home. They were wonderful, amazing dogs that required extra care, but I have chosen to work with special needs dogs. Luna had nine perfectly healthy siblings, and sadly, there are many more purebred dogs in need of rescue at high kill shelters throughout the country. It is truly heartbreaking. Personally, rescue is my favorite breed. Logan and his family were a mix of a few different types of dogs. This does not bother me, every animal in my home is loved.

When I rescued Luke, I was presented with his breeders' information, pedigree information and a bunch of other things to show he was considered a well-bred dog. That did not save him from his first 10 years of abuse and neglect. I have debated if I should send the breeder Luke's book, so he knows the hardships a puppy from his litter endured.

Since Luke embedded paw prints on my heart, I melt when I see a husky, especially if they have similar markings. If I did adopt another Husky, I would search all the animal rescue sites online first. Personally, I would not wait for a husky to arrive because there is always a dog in need of a loving home. There are purebred rescues in almost every state. High energy dogs such as; Siberian Huskies, German Shepherds, Belgium Malinois, and Cattle Dogs are frequently surrendered because of the time required to train them. When they have pent up energy and are bored they can become destructive, I have experienced this first hand. The dog can be perfectly healthy, just in need of patience and training, like all dogs. The saying *you cannot teach an old dog new tricks* was debunked by dog trainers as soon as it was created.

I have had people approach me asking my opinion on if they should breed their dog. My response is always the same, "Can you truly guarantee, a puppy from your litter will be a family pet? What if they have a life like Luke's? What if they end up with a backyard breeder, having an abundance of puppies until they're sick?"

Dog Breeding

As much as I would love to see everyone rescue a dog versus use a breeder, dog breeders will exist. Yet the more backyard dog breeders that can be shut down the better. Sadly, the parents of these puppies have many health problems because they are bred, too often, primarily for the owner to make money. I shared above the experience I had with one breeder.

I acknowledge that some dogs are intentionally bred for specific jobs; military duty or for specific medical issues such as brace and mobility dogs. In some states, there are specific laws with detailed standards the dog must meet to be able to help the individual. Some locations have breed specifications as well. Over the past few years, Great Danes have been recognized to assist taller individuals with medical needs. This breed is usually not found in shelters and are not commonly bred.

I have worked with many trainers who have pulled dogs from shelters and trained them to work with police. Some of their dogs now work with search and rescue teams throughout the United States. I believe in time all states will acknowledge that rescued dogs can give back and serve their community. I understand not all rescued dogs can do this. I love Lucy with my whole heart, but I am realistic in stating she would never be able to work for the local police department. It would be a huge waste of tax-payers money.

If individuals are seeking a pet, PLEASE consider adoption first. If one still prefers to go to a breeder please thoroughly research the breeder. Learn about the health of both the mother and father dog. Ask about the pups' diet and how many shots the puppy had. Lastly, please make sure the puppies are not being taken from the mother too soon. A dog will bond with their owner and be able to learn training commands with patience. Mothers and puppies being kept together for at least eight weeks IS the healthiest option for the puppies.

Chapter 15

More friends, More Fun

When I returned home without Luna, Logan looked around for the first day. He remained entertained because his brother Buddy was staying with us for a week. Luna annoyed Lucy, so she was relieved to have the house quiet again and was happy her son Buddy was visiting.

After Buddy went back to my mom's house, I fostered another little puppy that I named Love Love. I wanted her to go to a loving home. All her siblings had gotten adopted very quickly, and she was the only one left. She was laid back, innocent, trusting, and calmly adjusted to all situations that arose. Luckily, she found her forever home in two weeks. But those two weeks were crazy, I was thankful nothing stressed her out. My friend who lived in Miami had to evacuate to my house with her pets. There were 10 animals, and 2 people.

I had pre-made hurricane treats if the storm did hit, but fortunately, it missed us. Within the same week of my friend leaving Love Love found a great home, and had a 7th grader as her new best friend. I see pictures of her online, and she is winning awards in obedient school. The family came to my house to meet her and fill out the adoption forms. As I sat with my foster's new mom completing the adoption paperwork, her son happily played with his new furry friend. By the time we were done, Love Love had her new collar and leash on her and without looking back walked out of my house and got into her new car. Her new mom said to me, "Do you want to say good-bye?"

With a smile on my face I said, "It's okay, I know she is in great hands, I don't want her to look back."

Logan and Love Love

Give me Grace

Logan was a bit jealous to see his friend get a car ride without him but I took him for one shortly after they left. I did not take in another foster because I had started to promote my first Love from Luke book. My friend was hosting a book gala for local authors, and offered me a table. The night of the book signing was soon approaching, and I was getting nervous. My three dogs did not help the situation. The day started very smooth. I had gotten my hair done and bought a new dress that I ironed the morning of the event. My car was packed with the books and some charm bracelets I made. I thought I had given myself enough time, but my dogs' agenda, and my agenda clashed that day.

I got out of the shower and was about to put on my make-up, when a friend called and asked what time the event was. I told her I was leaving the house within 10 minutes. As soon as Chimayo heard that he got up and jumped all over my new dress. He got dirty paw prints on it, plus he wrinkled it. Foolishly, I had just taken it out of the closet and laid it on the bed when the phone rang. I got off the phone, grabbed the dress, hung it on the shower pole and turned the shower on to steam the bathroom, hoping to get the wrinkles out.

Flustered, I left the room, only to find that Logan decided, today was the day he was going to take up chewing again. He had not chewed since Luna moved out, but today he pulled the fabric and stuffing out of the arm of my sofa. I was furious! Logan saw me hurrying toward the sofa and ran into the bedroom to be with his mom. What made me even angrier was he thought he was funny. He wagged his tail and playfully walked past me. Ugh!

This was the moment I ran into the garage and let out a big and frustrated yell, I was so mad. Then I came back into the house, while I was scolding the dogs, I started cleaning the living room. I do not remember exactly what I said, but it was something like this, "This is why dogs go to pounds. Are you doing this on purpose, to make dog rescue look bad? None of you are funny! You're just spoiled."

While I was picking the stuffing off the living room floor and yelling at my dogs someone pulled their car in behind me in my driveway. *Now what,* I thought to myself. One of my friends had wanted to drop off a picture for the table I would be at for the book signing. I took them from her, embarrassed I asked if she heard me frantically yelling at what my dogs did. "No," she said as she was going to sit down on the sofa for a visit.

    I looked at the clock and said, "I can't visit with you, I needed to leave 10 minutes ago. I am going to have to go to the venue like this and get ready once my table is set up."

    I was in workout clothes, and I had no make-up on. My friend hurried out and told me she would see me again in a couple hours. I ran into the steamy bathroom grabbed the dress, put my make-up in a bag, and frantically drove to the venue. Once my table was set up, I had a friend watch it and got ready in the bathroom. The night was really fun. There were no more mishaps the remainder of the evening.

Loved little Luna off to her loving forever home today, September 18, 2016.

Chapter 16
Hello Again

The day Luna got adopted I posted this picture on all of my social media sites. My life had become so busy I did not check on Luna as I should have. To this day I am still enraged at what happened in the 10-weeks that Luna was out of my care.

As I briefly explained before there was a man who wanted a German Shepard dog to be his very own. He had previously adopted a male German Shepard from the rescue. When he adopted the first dog, he took a one week vacation from work to bond with his new family member. The dog was loved so much he was included in professional family pictures.

The background on the family had already been conducted. I took Luna to visit them for a few hours a couple of days before her adoption. The entire family fell in love with how small and cute she looked. They posted about six videos on social media during her home visit. I was told through the rescue that Luna was approved to go the man, his wife, and two pre-teenage daughters.

I personally emailed and physically hand delivered all of Luna's medical work to this man. It included: medical shot records, emails from the vet explaining the specific care Luna needed, x-rays that had been taken of her spine, vet's instructions explaining why she needed to swim, and where she could have discounted acupuncture when needed. Plus, I provided a three week supply of the vitamins she was to be kept on to support her bones, muscles, and prevent her from struggling to walk.

The application had an additional page attached to it that myself and the man both initialed. A list of 12 addendums the man and his family promised to oblige. On top of that, two of the same applications were filled out so we would both have original copies.

While filling out the application and chatting about Luna, I showed the man the video of Luna and my dogs digging a hole in my backyard earlier that day. Luna got so dirty I needed to give her another bath. After that, I took a shower before taking her to her new home. While showering, Luna, Logan, and Buddy got themselves into even more trouble, and chewed Lucy's bed. All three dogs pretended to act guilty when I scolded them. Luna ran into the other room, but she was happily wagging her, she didn't feel bad about it.

The man and his family thought the videos were funny, but I was warning them that this is what he was getting himself into. When I dropped her off, he took me into his yard to show me his pool. I reminded him that Luna loves to swim and to be careful because she jumps in the pool on her own. He replied, "Oh, I am going to make her a special float for when she in the pool for her therapy!" But that never happened!

I left Luna in what I believe to be good hands. Looking back on that day, there were signs that I should have questioned more. Regretfully, I didn't. The first sign was I did not see any toys in the house for their first dog. Second, he haggled over the adoption fee and made a big deal over $25.00. Third, he said could not pay the adoption fee for two weeks because he was broke. Lastly, he did not take off and replace the collar and leash I had on her but kept mine. I know this may sound petty but being a foster I usually go to the dollar store for collars and leashes, they are not the best, but they work. Most people who adopt a dog are so excited about their new family member they spend the day before picking out; a new bed, toys, collar, leash, food, and doggie ID tags. Not this guy!

The day after Luna's adoption I got a phone call from the man stating that Luna woke them up at 2:00 a.m. crying. Well, first she is only 12 weeks old, she was a baby! I explained she was going through a growth spurt and was waking up wanting an extra bowl of food and stressed that her body needed it. I reminded him that I was giving her an extra bowl of food around 10:00 p.m. to hold her through the night.

I am not sure if he followed my recommendations, but I did not hear from him again for another 3 days.

The next time I was contacted was because he wanted to know why the tip of her ear was floppy. I explained she was born that way and it does happen to many dogs and cats in the birth canal. He then wanted to know if it would ever stick straight up like his other shepherds. I told him that he would need to ask his vet. I was confused by the question because Luna is to be loved for who she is, not for what is deemed flawed in show dog society.

The first month I saw many photos of Luna and her new brother at the park or in the backyard. I had taken in some new foster puppies so did not stay on top of communicating with the family about Luna. This will always be a huge regret of mine.

December 8, 2016, close to three months after Luna was placed in the care of this *supposedly* loving family, I got a call asking if I had disclosed Luna's 13th vertebrae to the family. The man said that his friends are commenting that she walked funny and wanted the rescue to take care of her medical bills. He claimed that I had given him a perfectly healthy dog and he was NEVER told she required medical care! He continued to argue that it was not disclosed on the adoption forms!

THAT BIG FAT LIAR!!! I was flabbergasted that there was any shock about Luna's condition. I explained that while Luna was in my care, she swam three times a week. One of the reasons she was adopted to this family was because he had agreed to continue to swim with her. I explained I gave him a supply of Logan's vitamins and stressed how important it was for her to have them. Logan's vitamins were beef scented and flavored; it was a powder that got sprinkled on the top of his food. Lastly, I told him where he could get a 4 month supply for $60.00. I explained that he could also get the highest dosage of vitamins at local stores, but she needed a specific amount per day.

Well that jerk (to be polite), angrily and accusingly DENIED everything! He claimed he was given a healthy dog that suddenly broke. I forwarded the rescue copies of the emails that had been sent to him on September 19, 2016, which included her x-rays. I explained that I sat down with him and went over the adoption forms and he initialed each addendum, I stressed we BOTH signed these. I gave them enough facts to go back to the big jerk, to protect the rescue and most importantly Luna. I told them I wanted Luna back, and I would go and get her that very day if needed. The rescue knew I was enraged. They did not want me to call him, but were going to inform him that they had signed copies of all the forms and emails from vets.

Two days later I received two text messages. The first was from Luna's big jerk adopter saying he wanted to return her. The second was from the rescue saying, "I hope you were serious about taking Luna back because the man doesn't want her!"

First, I spoke with the liar, he acted very sad and said that they did not feel they could give Luna the care she needed. I tried to be respectful, but in my mind, I was thinking - *Really! There are four of you in the house, you have two pre-teenage daughters and a wife, you CANNOT provide adequate care for a special needs dog.....No, the truth is none of you want to be bothered with caring for her! So you* will hand her back to me, who already owns three special needs to do it for you. Then tell people how your act of surrender was noble when you NEVER should have made the commitment, to begin with!*

After that, I spoke with the rescue. The man admitted that he took Luna off her vitamins the very first day he got her. He left the beef scented vitamins on the floor, she broke into the bag and ate them all at once. Then he went to the store and bought the cheapest and lowest dosage of the vitamins possible, and was giving her half a pill once a day. Compared to the six per day she was on at my home. I questioned if it was a money problem but the head of the rescue explained that he was a cheap and selfish man that did not deserve the love of any dog.

I asked if he was going to have his first dog removed from the house, but they said he treats his healthy dog like gold, they did not want to remove him. But the man was banned from adopting a dog from most reputable rescues in the state of Florida.

The rescue explained the man and his family wanted to keep her over the weekend. To this day none of us are sure why, I personally believe it was to try and trick us into thinking he was a nice guy, but no one was fooled.

Over the weekend I prepared for Luna's return. Monday, December 12, 2016, at 7:00 a.m., I received a text that he was driving Luna to my home. When he took Luna out of his cherry-red sports car, my heart sank and the blood drained from my face. I was furious and heartbroken all at the same time. It was hard to hold back my tears seeing her struggle to walk from the driveway into my house, watching her fall on the ground and wince after every few steps. My healthy loved Luna was sooo skinny and weak at six months old.

I asked how much she weighed and the monster responded 35 pounds. I could see and feel most of her bones, she had been starved. My poor Luna could only walk a few steps before her back legs would give out and flatten her to the ground. She would then struggle to get up. Her back feet were too weak to hold her up properly. Her back paws had cuts on the front of them from having to drag, and pull herself with her front legs while her back legs to dangle behind her. The fur above her paws was scrapped off. They were swollen with scabs on them.

Luna was perfectly portioned when she left my home. In three months a starved and neglected dog was being returned to me. Luna's abuser came over to my sofa and started to show me what he was returning of hers. He returned the dollar store collar, leash and the thin blanket I had given her when I regretfully left her with this selfish monster of a man. The family never took Luna shopping for new things. He said she fit into cheap collar until just last week. The man also brought three cans of random wet food that I learned had been donated to him by someone else. He did not bring any of the food that she was currently eating with him, meaning I would have to go out and get her new food when he left.

It was clear this family never purchased or went out their way to do anything kind or loving for Luna. Poor Luna with her sore legs and spine, was never been given a dog bed or fluffy blanket to rest on. She spent eight hours a day or more in a crate with the thinly quilted pillowcase I sent her with. I gave him the pillowcase to be placed on top of her new doggie bed so she would have a familiar scent as she adapted into her new home. Luna was put on that same food as their adult German Shepard. He never purchased puppy food to give her the nutrients she desperately needed. He had stopped giving her the required amount of glucosamine chondroitin for her muscles and bones. Luna went from 6,000 milligrams a day to 375 milligrams.

The vitamins I gave the family came in a powder to be mixed in with Luna's food, it smelled and tasted like beef, naturally she loved it. The same day I dropped Luna off at his house he left the bag of vitamins on the floor, Luna got into the bag, and ate all of them. He admitted he went to the drug store, but picked up the cheapest bottle of glucosamine chondroitin.

Confused, I said, "Why didn't you call me that day to ask about what she specifically needed? I gave you the website information to get a four-month supply!"

In my mind I thought, *You called me over something as stupid as her tipped ear, but you would not call me about how to keep her healthy!*

The man avoided my questions and refused to make eye contact. He went to see where Luna was. Luna had stumbled and staggered into my house the best she could. When she realized where she was, she went outside to see the pool she used to swim in. As she saw it her ears went back. Poor thing, I could tell she was shocked by her facial expression, a couple days before I learned she was returning I had drained the water out it. Later that week, I did fix it, so Luna could start her swimming.

The man went into my backyard as well. He stated that his pool was vinyl and he did not allow Luna in the pool because he did not want her to ruin it. At this point I could no longer hold back the anger in my voice or my facial expressions, I said very directly, "Why did you bother to adopt her when it was made clear she needed to swim for physical therapy? Why did you tell me you were going to do that for her but didn't? What happened to the special raft you were going to make for her?"

He was taken back by my confrontation. He quickly replied, "Well, I took her for lots of walks."

In a very sarcastic voice, I replied, "Great, exactly what the vets said not to do!"

He turned his head and looked a bit stunned while my piercing eyes glared at him. I starred him down without flinching. He did not want to make eye contact he walked into my house and suggested we fill out the surrender forms. This is the only time I can agree with anything he did for Luna. While completing the forms he said he never took Luna to the vet and wanted to know if he should put the vet information down for his other dog.

Annoyed again by his nonsense, I said, "Leave it blank, if Luna was not seen by him, I do not need to talk to him." *Thanks to your neglect she is now behind on her shots as well*, I thought to myself.

Once the forms were completed the man quickly said goodbye to Luna and left. Luna looked out the window briefly, maybe 25 seconds. She wanted to play with her first and good friend Logan. She came over to me, and I lifted her up on the sofa. I let Logan out of his bedroom, he joyfully came running toward her. I had put him in the other room while Luna was being returned. It broke my heart to see her get tired so quickly because she was so weak.

Once Luna was settled in I realized I needed to get her some of her the food she had been eating at the other house and then puppy food. I already had the vitamins to start her on because of Logan's dietary and medical needs, so that wasn't going to be a problem. I gave Luna the food I had in the house for now. She ate six cups, one right after the other. It was clear she had been starving. So much for the breakfast, he claimed to have fed her before she arrived.

Foolishly, after Logan and Luna finished playing, I allowed Luna to fall asleep on my tile floor. When she woke up, she was crying in pain and had even more trouble trying to walk. Ugh… now I was mad at myself too. I realized Luna was going to need an orthopedic bed to help soothe her achy joints and muscles.

The rest of my day was spent gathering items to help Luna heal physically and emotionally. While I was out shopping my mother allowed Luna to use one of her dogs' beds. When Luna went over to her house, she started looking at all the toys and took some into the bed with her. Luna tried to get up to go back to the toy box to get more toys, but she fell over and started to cry. I picked her up and placed her in bed with the toys she wanted. The soft bed must have felt good. She was finally able to rest comfortably. My mom's dogs Buddy and Faith would come over to her to give her kisses and affections. All the dogs knew Luna needed TLC, and they generously gave it to her.

Throughout the day and the next morning, I grew angrier than I can ever remember being in my entire life, I wanted to hit and kick the wall. I wanted to go back into my garage and scream swears at the top of my lungs, but that would only scare my household. I wanted to talk to people, but I knew most of my friends would want to cause trouble for the selfish monster that had hurt my poor Luna!

My anger flared even worse was when I went onto social media and saw the man who returned Luna posted pictures of new tires for his truck. He posted he felt he deserved a present for having to give up his dog! Then the weekend before he returned Luna to me, both the man and his wife posted a bunch of pictures of the beachfront hotel in Miami, FL where they vacationed. Included in the photos was a full bottle of champagne they ordered for breakfast mimosas and needed to show off.

I was beyond furious, what a horribly cruel, selfish and materialistic family Luna had the misfortune of spending three months with. They could not spend money on her vitamins, they couldn't even buy her a new collar or dog bed, but he spent money on fancy cars and champagne. They wanted Luna because they thought she was pretty, that she would fit into their superficial lifestyle and when she was flawed they returned her. It sounded over and over again my head; *What's wrong with her ear? My friends are making comments on how funny Luna walks.* I had never been so disgusted in my life. How shallow! I wanted vengeance, and I wanted it badly.

I kept thinking about the thick silence that occurred when he refused to answer the direct questions I asked; *Why didn't you call me the day she ate all her vitamins? Why did you not take her swimming? Why, why, why would you let a healthy dog who was a little different suffer! Why was she never seen by a vet or put on puppy food? Why did you do this to a poor innocent puppy with special needs?*

For my own emotional health, I blocked him, his wife, mother and daughters from ever being able to contact me again. They had no rights, to Luna! I did not want them near her or to know anything about her!

To worsen my anger, friends would make comments about being mad about the condition Luna was returned to me in. They asked me who the man was, and shared what they would have done to him out of rage when she was returned to my house. I wholeheartedly agreed with them, I would try to shake it off by saying, "Yes, I am hurting and upset, but I have to focus on getting Luna healthy again. I need to forget about the family that abused and neglected her."

Regardless, of how often I would say it out loud or to myself, the anger was festering inside me. I wanted to get rid of it, but didn't know how. It was true I needed to focus on getting Luna healthy again. But, forgiving and forgetting what this man did to my foster puppy was immensely hard for me. Daily I watched her struggle to walk, mending a dog that never should have been broken.

On a daily basis, I would track Luna's progress, her small improvements, but did not post anything on my social media pages. The main reason being was many people wanted to know why Luna was back with me, and why she was in such bad shape. As much I wanted everyone to know how cruel the man and his family were, in the long run, it would not help Luna to heal. It would not help anything. Healing Luna had to be my main focus. Much like it was with Luke, I had to be emotionally and spiritually healthy. I had to have a positive, loving attitude toward every aspect of her life. I needed to move forward and forget her horrible past.

The first day I had Luna she was happy to see me, Logan and her other friends, but she was also scared and confused. She wanted to be very close to me. Luna had a long skinny body, she was only 35 pounds. I carried her when she could not walk or when she would cry for me. I would lay her on my sofa we would snuggle, and read or watch TV together. Logan understood she needed extra love too. He was always kissing the sores on her paws and bringing her toys. Luna was finally receiving the love and care she always should have had.

As the days progressed it was clear Luna was happier and within a week she was able run to me without falling when I called her. She did develop a bit of an ego. With each small improvement, the received praise was over the top. Luna had no problem accepting the admiration and was beginning to thrive again.

Yet, Luna did other things that made it clear that she had not only been neglected and denied food, but she had been physically abused. If Luna and Logan got into mischief, and I told them to stop Luna would drop on the floor, try to find something to hide under, and wet all over herself. She was petrified of my stern voice. This broke my heart and worsened my anger. Even if I scolded another dog, she would hide under my table, and her whole body would shake. I would move the chairs from the table and get on the floor to pull Luna onto my lap. Sometimes she wet herself, sometimes she wet on me, but it didn't matter. What mattered was showing Luna she was loved, and mending all her wounds both physically and emotionally. I had to consistently reassure her it was okay.

Luna never hid, wet on herself or physically shook when she heard a stern voice at my home or her previous foster home. Luna's only way to communicate what had happened to her was to demonstrate fear and overly submissive behavior.

Now, I was dealing with four issues. First, I had to figure out a diet to get her muscle tone back and get her healthy again. Second, I needed to help Luna overcome being neglected and emotionally abused. Third, I now needed to help Luna overcome the physical abuse she endured. Fourth, I need to get a grip on my own grief and resentment over Luna's condition.

Chapter 17
From Bad to Worse

Luna was making exceptional progress for the first 10 days of her return. Every day, she was getting happier and healthier. Yet, one day when she got off the sofa I noticed her front leg twist slightly inward, and she was favoring it. Just great I thought, this poor dog has problems walking with her hind legs, and now she has a problem with her front leg as well.

I called the rescue and told them I thought Luna hurt herself playing with Logan. That did not go over to good, but they agreed Luna should to go to the vet. She needed to get up to date with her shots anyway.

I dropped Luna off at Dr. Charlie's. Everyone in the vet's office greeted her with sincere excitement which pumped up her spirits. She cheerfully walked into the back room with the vet tech.

A few hours later Dr. Charlie called me. He said Luna was going to need to spend the night. She did not hurt herself from playing with Logan. Horrifically, her body was deteriorating from the lack of vitamins and nutrients she was denied while in the adopters' home.

With all my heart I believe Dr. Charlie refused to say the word neglect or abuse, for fear of what I and everyone who loved Luna would have done to the people that hurt her. Instead, he said it was evident that Luna received *sub-minimal care* while she was away from me. Dr. Charlie repeated the word sub-minimal about three times during our conversation. In my opinion, there is no difference between the word neglect, abuse or sub-minimal care when it comes to providing a loving home for an animal, child, senior or any living creature.

It was then explained, that Luna needed to be hooked up to an IV to pump her body full of the required vitamins and nutrients she had been denied. She was going to be closely monitored for at least six months to determine if she would need spinal surgery. There was a chance that by age five, Luna would be in a doggie wheelchair.

I was silently crying on the other end of the phone while I listen to what Dr. Charlie was saying to me. My face was on fire with anger and guilt. The tears were streaming down my face so rapidly the top of my shirt was wet. But I could not make a sound, I was brokenhearted and speechless. My body physically ached, my stomach hurt from the anger, stress, sadness, and confusion I was feeling toward myself, Luna, and her abuser all at the same time. It was agreed that Luna would stay in the doggie hospital until her vitamins and nutrient levels were up.

When I got off the phone, I called Ellie, I was so upset my voice was cracking, and my body was shaking. I hated myself, I truly hated myself for not proactively checking in on Luna and leaving her with a cruel monster for three months. Because of me this poor dog may need major surgery, and be permanently crippled. I spent months beating myself up over this.

Ellie did her best to comfort me. She introduced me to a group that makes special blankets for sick and abused dogs. The group asked me to share Luna's story and once she received the handmade blanket to share updates. While Luna was in the hospital, she received two extremely special blankets filled with prayers requesting that she would be blessed with a miraculous healing.

When Luna was released from the hospital, she was exhausted. She was very still and did not want to be petted or to play with Logan. I set up my guest bedroom for her. She got right into her bed and would lie on top of one prayer blanket. I covered her up with the other one. I know these blankets comforted her because she never tried to take them off her. It was as if the prayers said over the blankets were being absorbed into her body.

For the next week, Luna slept the majority of the time and sought to be alone in the guest room, in her bed with the blankets. I kept the door shut so she would not be disturbed. She would cry for me when she wanted attention or to go to the bathroom. I would sit on the floor with her and read books, while petting her, in hopes of comforting her. It is amazing how animals can communicate with one another. Logan understood Luna was sick and was extremely respectful of her desire to be left alone. When he did see her, he did not initiate play, but kiss her face and sit next to her. Watching this was uplifting. I was proud to have adopted such a caring young puppy.

Luna- Your Name Means Strong

On a daily basis, I watched Luna slowly progress and I became overly of protective her. I wanted to ensure she did not injure herself playing or trying to do something she used to be able to do. Yet, at the same time I would remind her that her name meant strong. That she was my invincible, fearless warrior, who could overcome anything. Sometimes, I would just call her my strong girl! I believed that the more I told her she was strong and healthy the faster it could be manifested. Plus, people from all over the country were praying for Luna to receive a miracle.

Refusing to say Abuse

However, Dr. Charlie's statement *"It very clear Luna received sub-minimal care, while in her adoptive home,"* lingered in my mind. I looked in the dictionary to learn the definition of sub-minimal care and compared it to what experts had stated abuse was, when I wrote the first Love from Luke book.

The words subminimal care could not be found as a definition, but I was able to find the word sub-minimal. According to the Merriam Webster Dictionary sub-minimal is defined as: *smaller than the minimum that is required for a particular result.*

This is clearly the definition of abuse! In my previous book *Love from Luke: Lessons learned from a Rescued Dog,* chapter 9 is dedicated to explaining what abuse is.

Neglect

One of the many facets of abuse is neglect. A neglected animal may have faced starvation, been denied shelter, and/or had little to no physical contact. Neglect also constitutes not having their basic needs met such as: grooming, vaccinations, and medical exams.

Luna was clearly abused! She was denied all medical treatment including her last set of puppy vaccinations. Her behavior toward food indicated she had not been fed enough to sustain her body. She may need spinal surgery and end up in a doggie wheelchair! There is no way to tiptoe around the fact the Luna endured three months of abuse.

Recognizing Symptoms of Abuse

Dogs that have been abused can demonstrate aggressive behavior toward humans because they do not understand love, kindness or had a good experience with human contact. Often times their body language is of cowering and some dogs will growl and show their teeth. They are not trying to scare the person, but are in fear or being hit, kick or God knows what else. They are trying to encourage the person to leave them, even if the person has the best intentions. These dogs require the most patience and love and often times some extra yummy dog treats and food for them to associate something positive with human interaction.

Other dogs who have faced extreme abuse will demonstrate Lucy's mannerism. Lucy will physically withdraw, keeping her tail between her legs, her head down and if she can hide, she will, especially when she is introduce to new situations. For a long time she feared seeing my hands reach toward her, in an attempt to pet her. When she walks pasts me, I often place my hand at her body level, so she walks under my hand, and I sort-of pet her. When I do this, she hurries past me. I still believe Lucy, will allow me show her affection, besides when she is scared of the vet.

If the dog is very fearful, he/she may start wetting on themselves as a sign of submission. Additionally, they may try to hide in a safe place to protect themselves from being physically abused.

This is how Luna behaved since returning to my home. It is clear Luna faced scary, stressful, and fearful experiences while at the other house.

The good news is Luna, Lucy and all dogs that have faced abuse can emotionally heal. It requires patience and love when working with an abused animal, but it *is 100 % possible* for the animal to know love and give love again. I have been fortunate to witness this first hand with every dog that has arrived at my home and the homes of my animal rescue friends.

**To fully understand all spectrums and signs of abuse in dogs please refer to Love from Luke: Lessons Learned from a Rescued Dog chapter 9. Topics discussed: Intentional Harm/Physical Cruelty to an Animal, Emotional Abuse, Recognizing Symptoms of Abuse, and Bullying

Chapter 18

An Angel & Devil on my Shoulder

While Luna was healing, I was struggling with my own rage and desire to seek vengeance on her abuser. For weeks it was as if I was walking around with an angel on one shoulder and a devil on the other one. To be honest, the devil was more enticing and hard to resist. I would toss and turn all night, talking myself out of retaliating against the man and his family. I had many friends who wanted to know who he was. They would say, "Come on Melissa, just tell me his name, that's all I need, nothing will be traced back to you!"

It was so tempting! I am proud to say I refused to release his information, but wow, I really wanted to. My own creative mind was on fire with vengeful things as well. I wanted to write bad reviews on his company's website. Making things up such as; *when I met with him, smelled of booze and marijuana cigarettes, and he kicked my Chihuahua!* I know this sounds funny, but this nonsense would not bring about anything positive.

Finally, one morning during my prayer and meditation, I was granted the realization as to why retaliating against Luna's abusive family was a waste of my time. I was reminded of when the zoo shot the gorilla after a child fell into his den. Individuals from all over the world reacted negatively toward the mother. As an animal rescuer, some sought my professional viewpoint on this matter. My perspective was unique from others and not very popular. I expressed how the past could not be changed. Nothing that was done after the gorilla was killed would bring him back. If all parties involved could change those few stressful moments, I believe everyone would have reacted differently. People act differently during moments of stress, and time cannot be rewound. I was personally upset with my observations about how violent and aggressive some animal rights individuals had become toward the injustice of the gorilla. People had become the bullies!

I was reminded of what I read in a Dali Lama book explaining how humans are not the strongest creatures on this planet sadly, we can be the most violent and aggressive. If I gave in to my anger and acted negatively toward Luna's abusers in any way, I was going to become and create bullies. Public shaming and bullying would not solve anything.

Luna would not be healed physically or emotionally. Her abuser agreed to surrender her versus keep her in an unhealthy situation. I had blocked them from finding out about Luna. Any negative retaliation would encourage my friends, and I to become hypocritical tormentors. Finally, after months of constant prayer to resist the temptation to retaliate, I no longer felt the pull or urge to publically humiliate or cause shame to the man and his family.

Luna did not think or care about them anymore. She was happy to have been returned to me. She was welcomed back into my home with an overwhelming amount of love and support. Releasing my anger and resentment felt incredible. My whole body felt better, I was thankful for the realization, but wish I could have had it sooner

Stronger Each Day

As I emotionally healed, Luna was also making incredible progress. Dr. Charlie and his family would see Luna when she visited my mother's house. She was slowly gaining weight, and her upper body was getting stronger. She was able to lift herself up onto the sofa and other pieces of furniture without any help. This was such a big deal to everyone who loved her that we cheered at just about everything she did. Of course, all the praise went straight to Luna's head.

Luna was getting her self-confidence back. Any place we went Luna had a strut in her walk, onlookers would smile and praise her too. We were excited that she was getting stronger and was actually able to go for short walks. In Luna's mind, all the cheers she received made her believe she could do no wrong. This later became a problem.

Three months after Dr. Charlie said she was going to need spinal surgery she was given a clean bill of health. Once again I was told that if Luna stayed on her diet with high dosages of vitamins, she would live a long and healthy life without surgery. When I got the news this time, my eyes filled with tears of joy. The prayers from all over the nation had been heard and Luna received her miracle.

After that, she was able to start going to adoption events. This was hard for me, considering everything I had gone through with her, I had become an overprotective foster dog mom. The rescue agreed that there would be an open adoption. My friend volunteered to come with me when it was time for Luna to go to her new forever home. The adoption events were a success, Luna enjoyed being a socialite. Many people wanted to get their picture taken with her because of how pretty she looked. Naturally, Luna loved all the attention. She would do different poses for the people taking her picture. The crowd watching her would go "Aaww, so cute!" "She's so adorable," and "What a little princess."

In my heart, I felt Luna was ready for her new forever home. Although I loved her, I believed she was angry at me for allowing that family to abuse her. As Luna got better, she started to act out. She became one of the most destructive dogs I have ever had.

Anything that she passed and could grab to destroy, she did! When she was in the yard, she ran by my patio furniture. She grabbed the tag on the bottom an outdoor chair cushion, she yanked it so hard it ripped in half. She threw it on the ground when I yelled, "No!" but then she ran to the other tag in an attempt to ruin the next cushion.

She had no remorse for any of this. I would scold her saying, "What did you do? Who made this mess?"

Luna would just stand still, look straight at me and have no expression of remorse or fear. It was clear she had gained her confidence back and knew I would not hurt her. She attempted to destroy my dining room table and chewed one of the legs. I exchanged tables with my mother. If it had gotten ruined, I would have been upset. I really liked my dining room table, but with Luna's mischief, I needed eyes on every side of my head. I was being as vigilant as possible, but Luna would run, find a string or tag on something and pull it with her teeth as hard as she could.

I had to get rid of my sofa and love seat from her destruction. I cannot say that was just from her, Logan had gone through a chewing phase and would join in if he thought he would not get in trouble. At least Logan comforted me in some way by pretending to be sad when he got caught.

Luna and Logan busted for attempting to eat the sofa

The first time the couch was chewed, I did a do-it-myself repair, purchasing stuffing and new fabric to cover the damage. Yet, this did not do the trick. If one was to look closely, they could see a few bumps in the newly glued fabric on top of the old fabric. Luna instantly found this and ripped the sofa armrest down to the wood. She was not ashamed of what she did. I would sternly say, "Did you do this?"

Luna would look me in the eye, she had no shame about what she did, and if she could talk to me, I am sure she would have said, *yeah, so what!* The days of her wetting on herself, shaking and hiding under the table were long gone.

I did not think Luna would ever be able to forgive me because of how bad her first adoption was. I believed it was in both our best interest if she was rehomed. Luna's new parents would have to take her to dog training classes, although Luna loved my dogs, she had no interest in making new friends. When Luna encountered a new dog her personality instantly changed. The hair on her back would go straight up, she would bark and show all her teeth. Her body language made it clear she did not want another dog around her. In dog language, I believe she was saying, *"Get out of here, this pact is full, and we do not want you to be a part of it."*

This left me wondering if Luna was deemed the *bad dog*, and the other dog was considered the *good one*. Was she stuck in a crate and watched the family love on the other dog in front of her?

These are questions I am never going to truthfully have the answered. I need to rely on my experience, and the mannerism of Luna, to make an educated assessment.

Let Sleeping Dogs Lie

Although I had moved on from what happened to Luna, for my own emotional well-being, I stopped going to the adoption events. Luna's abuser showed up at one of the places, plus he contacted me on a new social media site I had set up. He even commented underneath pictures of her, stating how awesome she was, and that he missed her. These statements set my rage toward him ablaze. I explained to the rescue that even though I knew he could never harm Luna again, I did not trust myself in his presence. I was honestly afraid I would retaliate and end up getting arrested.

When he contacted me on social media, I really thought it was going to get out of hand. I started posting pictures of Luna when she was healthy and ready for adoption. My friends saw Luna's struggles, plus I had shared the private videos of Luna falling over and wincing in pain when she first returned. When her abuser posted he missed her, it was clear that this was the man who caused her so much harm.

Naturally, all of this had to happen when I was at a dog rescue event promoting my first book. I had a friend from Philadelphia call me at my fundraiser. When I answered the phone, the first thing she said to me is, "Wow, that man is stupid!"

I did not know what she was talking about. Then she told me, the man was commenting on photos of Luna. To make matters worse, another friend posted underneath what the abuser said with "Gotcha!"

If I didn't take care of this now, there was going to be trouble. I had to excuse myself from my book promotion to block the man and his family from being able to see Luna on another new social media page. I had to call the rescue and have them do the same thing. Then I called my friend, calmed him down and pleaded with him not to retaliate or have his friends do anything. Out of respect for me, he promised to leave the man alone and let sleeping dogs lie.

The rest of my book promotion was ruined. Usually, I enjoy speaking with people and hearing stories about their rescued pets. My favorite thing is to see the before and after pictures of the family pet. That day, I just wanted to be at home and hug Luna. I also wanted to scream in anger at the top of lungs. Once again, my mind filled with revenge schemes against the family who exposed Luna to cruelty. This man wanting to be in our lives was a struggle for me. I just wanted to focus on Luna and my other dogs' well-being in peace. I had refused to see or speak to the man. It had been made clear to him that I wanted to be left alone and did not want him near Luna. Yet, he continued to disrespect my request.

The rest of the day my mind was absent. The angel and devil reappeared on either side of my shoulders. Both of them were whispering in my ears, and they both had good arguments.

The devil said:

Melissa, you have been keeping this secret for far too long. All you have to do is say two words, and it will all go away. Once you let the secret out, you will feel so much better. Remember everything he did? He doesn't care at all. He keeps bothering and disrespecting you. All you have to do is say two words, and you'll be left alone. Your life will be peaceful again. Isn't that what you want? People are losing respect for you, they think you are nuts protecting this guy. Just tell them who hurt Luna, and everything will stop. Give them the name of the man who hurt Luna, just tell them, you know you want to! Wouldn't it be nice to have a peaceful night sleep versus tossing and turning with your nightmares about dog abuse? Simply release the name!

The angel said:

Melissa, you have been entrusted to keep two words to yourself. If you say the name of the person who hurt Luna, YOU will cause people to do things in anger that they will later regret. You will turn nice people into tyrants. Far more people will be hurt worse than you can ever imagine if you give out his name. This is hard, but protecting this man from harm is the right thing to do. Luna is getting better, ignore him and keep your focus on her.

When I got home, I showered all my dogs with extra love. I went on a massive workout binge to release my anger and then laid in bed feeling completely defeated again. All the forgiveness I had finally established I felt had been trampled on. Later that evening I decided to write him a letter of everything I wanted to say to him, but at the same time I wanted nothing to do with him.

I want to Forgive & Forget All about You!

To Luna's Former Family,

You need to stop contacting us, wanting to be in Luna's life or thinking you have right to Luna! She is legally with me. I will fight with every ounce of my being to protect her from you and heartless people like you.

I am not sure if you know this about me, but I used to be a college professor. I taught three classes on conflict resolution. The number one thing I would stressed upon my students was for them to learn exactly who they are, and to identify what issues in this crazy world bothered them the most. Whatever topic or issue enraged them, and made their blood boil, was not a conflict that would be fairly resolved.

Animal abuse is the issue that makes my blood boil! Therefore, it is best for all parties involved that you stay away from Luna and me. I am disgusted that you have the nerve to think it is okay to visit her when your wife has told several people I know that she <u>did not like Luna!</u> I will never understand why you kept her so long and allowed her to suffer.

It is legally documented that while in your care Luna suffered. Although Luna cannot speak, it's clear that besides the fact that you admitted to denying Luna her required food, vitamins and physical therapy, she endured physical abuse. There is no reason that when Luna hears a stern voice for her to fall on the ground, wet on herself, and hide under a table. There is no excuse I will EVER accept from anyone to harm an animal, especially a 12-pound crippled puppy!

The instant you or someone in your household wanted to hurt Luna was the instant you should have picked up the phone and called me. I will never accept any excuse you have for not calling me. I would have removed her from your home within the hour. That would have been the kindest thing you could have done for her, but instead, you felt justified in harming a crippled puppy.

Flat out when you hurt Luna you shattered my heart into a million pieces and then poured acid all over it. Every second of watching Luna struggle to walk, wince in pain or wet on herself, poured more salts into the wounds you gave me. It is ONLY by the GRACE OF GOD that I protected you and your family from being publically shamed for the harm you caused Luna. Regardless of all the pretty shiny material things you possess, it does not take away from the fact that you have a dark and hallow soul that both Luna and I know about.

Luna is going to get better, and she is going to have a positive impact on this world. I am not sure what she is going to do, but I know it's special. I selected a name that meant strong on purpose. I know she will be victorious because she is now surrounded by love and prayers. My anger toward you does Luna no good. She has arrived at my house and has never looked back at her past with you. Luna is happy and striving again, the rest of her life Luna will experience happiness. I know she is meant for very big things.

If you have any love for Luna, you will stay away from us. I want to forgive you and every time I feel I have reached forgiveness you show up and create nothing but drama. Not for Luna, but for *everyone who truly loves her and was hurt by what you and your family did to her.*

Again, please leave us alone so we can effectively forgive and forget Luna's past!

***

I never sent this letter, but ironically getting everything out on paper did the trick. No one ever heard from Luna's adoptive family again. Not only was Luna able to get better, but I was able to become emotionally healthy too!

As the time passed, I was finally able to forget about Luna's adoption. I know Luna never thinks about it, she's very happy. I have forgiven the family, the best I can. I never want to see them again, but if our paths crossed, I believe I could be diplomatic toward them, if I did not have Luna with me. If she was there, I would have to walk away, and quickly.

What I learned when trying to forgive and forget about Luna's past is just how tricky and how many disguises the devil has. A year had passed since I wrote the letter to Luna's brief home. I had completely forgotten about what had happened to her. I was vending at a farmers market. At my table, I have photos of the dogs I have cared for. I have small explanations written below their pictures about their past and their new happy life. A man came to my table, he briefly looked at the items I was selling and said to me "What's his name?"

Confused, I said, "Who are you talking about?"

He pointed to the picture of Luna and said, "Who was it who hurt this dog? What's their name?"

I was taken back, no one had ever read my dog's story and wanted to know who hurt them. I had only been asked how the dogs are currently doing. In a surprised voice, I said, "I don't know, I know Luna is very happy, and that is what matters."

The man did not believe me, he leaned in on my table toward me and said, "Are you telling me you do not know the name of the person who hurt this dog? If you tell me the name, I will give you $1,000.00, right here, right now!"

I know I was surprised, and the man was serious, he was going to give me $1,000.00 to release the name of the person who hurt Luna. I tried to reply in a nonchalant manner saying, "You can buy $1,000.00 of the products I am selling, and I can leave the event early today."

The man looked me dead in the eye, it was clear he understood that offering a $1,000.00 to an animal rescuer is a big deal. I was thinking about how many animals I could spay and neuter. Again, he said, "No, I don't want any of your things, I'm not interested in them. I really want to know who hurt this dog. I will take care of it. I think people who hurt animals should have the same thing done to them. Don't you agree?"

I was silent, I know I looked surprised and wide-eyed. The man once more offered me $1,000.00. He was sly about it too, saying, "I know your rescue could use the money. Charities know how to make a small bit of money go a long way. You want the money too, I know you do, so just tell me!"

At this point I got annoyed some of my anger could have been because he hurt my pride when he stated he did not like anything I was selling. I felt manipulated and patronized. In disgust, I shook my head and said, "You have to leave my table, you are preventing other people from making real donations or looking at what is for sale. You have to go."

The man said a few more things. He really wanted me to agree that it was okay to seek vengeance on animal abusers. Finally, in a firmer voice I said, "I have forgiven and usually forget all about the dogs past. I have to care for them, not chase down the people who hurt them. They know in their hearts what they did was wrong. Guilt and regret are horrible emotions all on their own. You have to leave, I have to work!"

Begrudgingly the man walked away, but he did swing by my booth a few more times to briefly tell me he thought I was insane for refusing his offer.

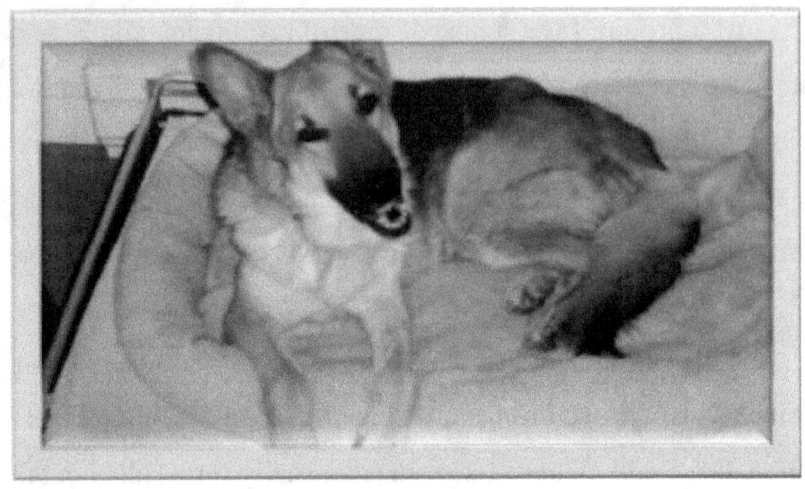

Chapter 19

Adam

Regardless of time, love has no boundaries
By Melissa A. Sweeney

When Luna needed to stay in the hospital for three days, I visited Ellie. She had collected donations for Luna. Her friend John had sent her a blanket that he wanted a special dog in need of love to have. Ellie felt Luna was the special dog who deserved this blanket. The only request was to send pictures of Luna using the blanket.

The blanket was warm and high quality. It was a beautiful color of red with white dogs on it. I received the blanket in December, so I told Luna it was a very special Christmas blanket filled with prayers and love. Luna was blessed with a second prayer blanket from another group Ellie introduced me to. I believe with all my heart, the prayers Luna received resulted in her miracle.

Luna's return from 3 days in the hospital

Yet, it was not until nearly six months later did I learn just how special this red blanket with the white dogs on it was. While I was going through my dog's medical records, I found a white envelope that had Ellie's name written across the front of it. I opened it to see if it was anything she needed. I found this letter written by John explaining the background, and the intention of the red and white dog blanket. I was so moved I called Ellie and asked her if she could introduce me to John. John is one of the most devoted and commendable dog heroes I have had the privilege to get to know.

Ellie introduced us via text message. I thanked him for Luna's blanket and asked if I could share the story his red and white blanket in this book you are currently reading. Because his dog Adam was so special to him, we both agreed Adam's story needs to be told to as many people as possible. I was granted permission to share the letter that came along with Luna's beautiful blanket.

Adam's Love Story

Hi Ellie,

Just wanted to give you a little history on our Adam, so you have an idea why this blanket is so very special to us. I got Adam on February 26th of 2015, and we lost him on March 1, 2015, just two days after I had him home.

I found out about him on a rescue site. He was hanging out of a broken window by his left rear leg at an abandoned home. Neighbors stated the family that owned him moved a week to 10 days earlier. They thought the family took Adam with them. He must have tried to escape from the home by jumping thru the window. The neighbor came home that afternoon and saw Adam was in trouble.

He was caught by his leg in the broken window frame. He was cut badly and bleeding. His hip had been dislocated. The A.C.O. (Animal Control Organization), along with the local Sheriff got Adam out of the broken window and took him to the vet. The neighbor did not know the folks moved and left him there or he would have taken Adam to his home.

Adam spent about a month at a local animal hospital. He was pretty bad. He had what was described as cuts to his rectal area, legs, and stomach. His hip was dislocated, and he was severely emaciated. He had constant diarrhea and wasn't gaining any weight. He was 43 pounds and should have been 70 pounds at least. The vets did all they could for him. Miraculously, his hip went back into place after a few days.

There was a rescue in Missouri that was going to take Adam. Adam was sent back to the shelter and awaited his rescue transport. Well after 10 days back at the shelter the rescue backed out for unknown reasons. I had stayed in touch with the A.C.O shelter on occasion.

I saw where he posted that Adam's rescue had fallen thru. I knew of a transport that was coming thru that area (Southern, Central Ohio on the Kentucky border of where Adam was) on the day I saw Adam wasn't to get rescued in Missouri. This was 8 o'clock on the evening of February 25th. The shelter folks could not get anyone to meet the transport near the interstate which was two hours away from the shelter. The transport guy I know called me at almost midnight and said he could not get Adam because of the inability of the shelter to assist in transporting Adam to him.

I started to scramble from there. At 2:00 a.m., just two hours after I was told he missed the transport I got into the Grand Cherokee. I had supplies, beds, food, blankets, and water on board and left for Southern Ohio, I drove 14 hours straight to get him, almost 800 miles. I live in Central Massachusetts. It was a very cold and snowy trip out there. I was exhausted when I arrived at 3:30 p.m. that afternoon on February 26th.

I went to the shelter, did the paperwork, and they brought Adam out of an old shed. He was in very bad shape, worse than I could have imagined. He was so cold; there was no heat in the shed, and it was 20 degrees that afternoon. He was covered in frozen poop, dirt and just a cold, emaciated mess. The floor in the shed was dirt and was also frozen. All he had was bottom of a dog crate to lie in. THAT'S ALL! He was so thin and shivering. I spent the next 20 minutes trying to clean him and get him warm. I was going to look for a place to stay overnight, but I wasn't sure Adam was going to make it. He was in bad shape overall. So at 4:00 p.m. that afternoon, just 30 minutes after getting him I decided to that I was going to drive straight thru and try to make it home.

I gave Adam some food and water, and we went on our way. I stopped only for fuel, to give him more food and water when needed, and for potty breaks. I kept checking on him all the way home. Adam was in a dog bed just behind my seat where I could reach back and feel him. I had him covered in blankets. The bed was very nice, orthopedic and soft. It was hours before he warmed up. It was another 15 hours' drive back home. We arrived at 7:00 a.m. on Saturday morning February 27th.

Adam slept most of the day. He was a very good pup, and when he came into the house, he woofed a few times as if he was happy to be there.

We had a special appointment for that Monday at our vet. He had come around pretty good during the night on the way home and thru the day on Saturday. I was fairly sure it was okay to wait until Monday. Getting warm and eating well seemed to help him a lot. If I had known Missouri rescue was going to back out, I would have gotten to him a lot sooner and not have let him stay at that shelter for 10 days freezing.

Adam slept a lot during the weekend. I always had a blanket over him to keep him warm. On Monday morning we let for the vet at

9:00 a.m. I dropped him off for the day and was going to pick him up the night of March 1st, after his tests and vetting.

My girlfriend works for the local police department, on that Monday morning, she had a friend from the district attorney's office visit. She told her friend about Adam and what had happened to him. She mentioned that he was almost frozen to death in the shelter and we had been keeping him warm all weekend with blankets and such.

Her friend then left, went to the pet supply store and bought Adam this beautiful, warm new blanket. He came back the same day and gave it to my girlfriend to give to Adam. So when Adam came home that night, he would have something from the heart.

That was the evening Adam did not come back home. Adam had slept in bed with me Saturday and Sunday evening. I kept him covered all the time to be sure he was warm.

This blanket bought by my girlfriend's friend has stayed in my closet for many months. Adam did not use it at all. He passed that Monday evening before he was able to come home.

The vet explained that Adam was suffering quite a bit. He had bi-lateral hip dysplasia so severe that his left hip would pop in and out of the socket as he walked. His intestinal tract had shut down, hence the constant diarrhea and the inability to gain weight. He had been starved for so long before he got hurt that there was no coming back from that. He had peri-anal fistulas that looked like lacerations, they were so horrible. His lower rectal area was paralyzed from the fistulas, and he did not receive treatment from his previous owner. The cuts were so deep, and his backside was covered with them. He had a lot of trouble moving his bowels. It took him almost 15 to 20 minutes each time he went. He could not feel when had to go or when he was finished going.

The vet and I had a long discussion as of the quality of life Adam was going to have going forward. It was not good, besides the fitulas, his body could not absorb any nutrition because his intestinal tract was close to shutting down and not working at all. Plus, Adam had a very painful dislocating hip. We decided the most merciful decision was to let him go. Both the vet and the ultrasound specialist agreed that this was best and prolonging Adam's suffering was not the right thing for Adam.

We said our good-byes Monday, March 1, at 9:45p.m. I have done rescue for German Shepherds for nearly 30 years. I have helped place and foster nearly 600 German Shepherd Dogs. Never in my experiences with rescue had I come across anything like Adam. I have never had to say goodbye in just two days of having a new dog in my home. This experience had broken me to the core.

I think I have seen too much, experienced all the pain and suffering I can take. I just can't seem to get past losing Adam. I now help where I can by donating to rescues, but I do not think I am ready to take on another case at this time.

We have five German Shepherds dogs, all rescues. Ikea is the oldest dog we took in Thanksgiving last year. He will be 14 years old next week. I know I have rambled here some and I am sorry for that.

I just wanted you to know a little history behind Adam. I also wanted you to have this blanket for a new "Baby Adam," for his comfort when he goes home. Maybe the foster mom can explain to

"Baby Adam's," new family the history behind this blanket. This is all I have left of his memory. That is why this is so very special for me to do this for another pup. I know Adam would want another pup to be warm and feel safe with his blanket that he did not get to use.

Thank you, Ellie, for all you do for those less fortunate,
Johnny

I know many of you will consider me this comment crazy but sadly, Adam is one of the lucky ones. Adam passed away knowing what true, undeniable love felt like. John, his girlfriend, the veterinarian, and friends all blessed Adam in his brief time with them. Much like my Luke, Adam died in a room surrounded by those who loved him and sought nothing, but his best interest. This is what Adam, and all dogs long for, to be loved. To have a best friend, and although Adam spent his entire life longing for this, the love did arrive, and just in time!

The truth is far too many dogs pass away alone, neglected and never knowing what love is. God did not design dogs to experience rejection and loneliness. They are genetically designed to be our companions. They have personalities, feelings, emotions and it has even proven that dogs do know how to smile and laugh.

I am pleased to announce that John is still active in animal rescue and continues to fight the good fight for their well-being. I know regardless of distance the blanket sent to Luna, filled with love and prayers brought comfort to her while she was healing. I also know that angel Adam is smiling down from heaven on John's kindness to Luna and the dogs he continues to help.

One thing people may not realize is once a person rescues an animal, they have basically joined a dog pact. Once they witness their first miracle, they become determined to heal the hurts of other animals too. In doing this the animal rescuer is blessed with so much love in their hearts, it's undefinable. Although we cry, and at times are in emotional agony from the cruelty we witness, we cannot imagine a life where we miss out on seeing the *happily ever after* stories that arise. Even if the animal passes away, we know their last few moments on earth were spent in loving and caring hands. We also acknowledge, some animals never even experience this.

Walking away from animal rescue means missing out on seeing the abused animal; first smile, show affection, wag of their tail, and the ability accept love and give love. If everything goes smoothly, we witness miraculous recoveries in the animal's physical and emotional state. Not to mention they find nurturing loving forever homes. We have the adoptive parents send fantastic pictures of them running in their new yards, relaxing in comfy beds and living a wonderful quality of life. Although it can be hard, the good parts of animal rescue do supersede the bad!

Chapter 20

On Our Knees

On St. Patrick's Day in March of 2016, the vets agreed that Luna was healthy. What a perfect day to receive the good news. She had rapidly defied all odds and would not need to have spinal surgery. Everyone was excited that our prayers for Luna had been answered and she was ready for adoption. The vets stressed again, that if kept on her vitamins she would live a long healthy and happy life. But our celebration of Luna was cut short.

Within a week of Luna getting the thumbs up from Dr. Charlie, Logan started limping. I had formed such a close bond with him, I knew something was wrong. We went to the vet, and the x-rays proved it. We were so focused on making sure that Logan did not shatter his front legs playing we forgot to pay attention to his back legs. Logan is good at masking pain because he does not want to miss out on any fun opportunities. The x-rays showed that the collagen in Logan's back left knee was gone (I am not a veterinarian, so will do my best to explain this as simply as possible). His knee was bone on bone, and the bones were rubbing together. The x-ray showed that Logan was misusing his back leg to protect his front legs. Fortunately, his front legs had healed, and he was able to be placed on higher protein food. This meant Logan had the expected recovery from panosteitis, we prayed for. This was happy news, but I would have preferred my puppy to have a perfect bill of health.

The bad news was Logan's was going to need to have a metal brace installed in his knee. This surgery is usually not performed on larger dogs, and the results may lead to Logan being in a wheelchair. I was not happy about this. In fact, I was sick of hearing bad news. I knew I needed to put Logan through the surgery. I did not take any time to think my decision over. I simply told Dr. Charlie to schedule the procedure. "Are you sure?" he asked with a bit of concerned at how quickly I agreed to it.

"Yes, if there's any dog that will overcome this, it's a dog of mine. Come on, you've witnessed first-hand my dogs' defy every obstacle they have come up against. Logan will do the same!" I believed this whole-heartily. At this point in my experience with the dogs I fostered, I had witnessed them overcome so much that I had no fear of Logan going through a surgery that was rare.

After I said it, Dr. Charlie and I both started to laugh, we knew it was true. If any dog could go through this, and come out victorious, it was one of mine. I schedule the appointment for Logan, but then called the office about three days later to move the surgery up. Logan was declining quickly. He loved to be outside and around people, but he was confining himself to his crate. He would eat, go to the bathroom, and go right back to bed. I understood the surgery needed to be done sooner versus later.

Bright and early on a Tuesday morning, in the middle of March, Logan received a metal knee. He fully understood what was happening. I even posted a video online trying to give him a pep talk about his knee. I was very cheery, saying "Who is going to defy all odds and get better really quick? YOU!" Logan would smile.

Then I would say, "Who's my brave boy getting a knee surgery? YOU!"

When I talked about surgery, Logan would make a somber face and look away from the camera. It was endearing.

Many people offered words of encouragement and prayer. A few hours later I got the good news that the surgery was a success and I could visit Logan. He needed to stay in the hospital for four days to rest and be observed. Each visit I would sit next to his crate and would give him a new special dog treat. On the second visit, Logan was allowed out of his crate. He needed assistance to walk, but once he was out, he walked past me to lie down next to another dog who was in a crate about five feet away. The dog in that crate was very big, too big for the crate. One of the vet techs must have understood what I was thinking and said, "This is Big Guy, he is in the crate, so you can visit Logan. When you leave Big Guy will come out and walk around again. Since Logan came out of surgery, he has been sitting next to his crate to comfort him."

Wow, I was overwhelmed at how cool it was to witness that level of compassion and comfort the dogs were giving each other.

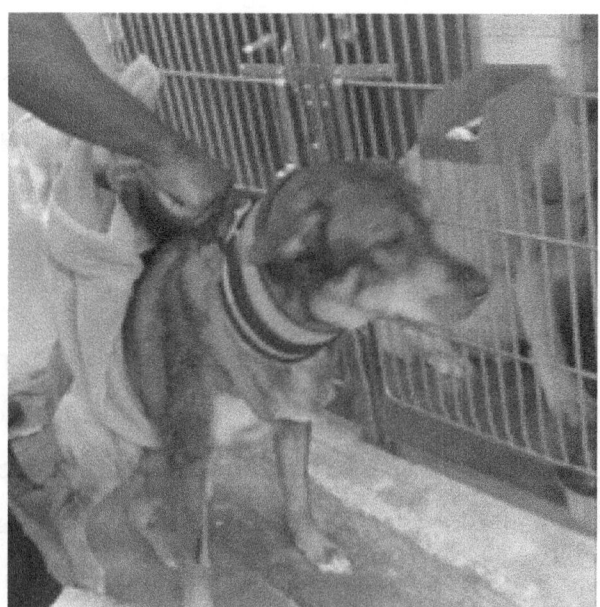

Logan and Big Guy

When Logan came home, his recovery was hard for me to handle. It was much harder than I expected it would be. The first few days Logan needed help walking and going to the bathroom. Logan being 90-pounds and me having back problems cause the two of us a great deal of pain. Logan needed to wear a waist brace to help hold him up when he walked. Most of the time these braces are really helpful, but Logan did not like it. He fought with me when I tried to put it on him. I was afraid trying to get the waist brace on could cause him to get hurt worse than he already was. Dr. Charlie stressed that this surgery is very rare for large dogs and proper rest for healing was essential. It was easier to get a towel around Logan's waist than the brace. This was more comfortable for him but harder for me to pull and hold him up with, when he needed to go to the bathroom.

Luna was young and wanted to play with him. She was finally healthy and could do things that she could not do before. I was on constant alert, trying to prevent Logan from getting hurt. When Luna saw Logan, she would run at him as fast as she could, and sometimes knock him over. The whole situation was frustrating, and I felt defeated. I knew Luna did not understand, but I wanted her to. I wanted her to comprehend that Logan could have permanent knee damage from her knocking him over. I explained to my mentor, I knew Luna did not want to harm him, she only wanted to play, but I was concerned I could not love her the same if Logan got hurt. I decided to get care for Luna, so Logan could heal from his surgery in peace. But to add to my stress, my pet sitter backed out, last minute. She said Luna was too active, and she needed to leave her home right away. I had to stop what I was doing, drive to the sitter's house, and bring Luna back to my house. Luna was now a healthy and active dog, a bit too active at times.

What made this situation even worse was I had agreed to drive a friend visiting me to Miami, Fl. I was planning to take 2 days to visit Roger and his family as well. Now the day of the trip my pet care completely fell apart. This made me feel even more disheartened, I was really looking to forward to having a break. It was too expensive for my friend to book a flight or train last minute to Miami so we still drove there. Then I had to drive straight back the same day, because the pet-sitter cancelled last minute we left for Miami late in the day causing us to hit all the traffic. I got home 12 hours later, I then needed to feed, let my dogs out to the bathroom, and exercise them before being able to go to bed.

Once everyone in my household was cared for, I opened a letter from the company I had a contract with. It explained they had filed for bankruptcy, and their contractual employees would not be receiving their last month of pay. I was upset, but I was so tired I could not get emotional. I put my dogs in their crates and went to bed. I slept soundly for a solid eight hours until the dogs started to make noise for their dinner and playtime.

Lucy, Chimayo, and Logan went back to bed after eating. They understood I was tired and accepted today was going to be a lazy rest day. This went over Luna's head. All she cared about was having a good time. She was feeling better than ever, and was confused by her friend's lethargic behavior. I wanted so badly to be able to have a serious talk with her and explain why she needed to be gentle. Instead, I would harshly yell at her if, I was not quick enough to keep her away from Logan. Luna was fast, too fast for me.

In a depressed state, I played fetch with Luna. I should have been pleased that she was able to sprint, wag her tail and was ecstatic to be playing a game with me, but my emotions were flat. Looking back, I often wonder if this hurt Luna's feelings. I reminded myself of how the puppies would cry to go to the bathroom all hours of the night and I would say to myself, *it's okay, this will not last forever*, but in my current mood that offered no comfort.

When Luna was finally tired we came inside, I passed the letter about my contract having to be canceled and not getting paid. What horrible timing! The same week I paid for Logan's new knee. What a bunch of inconsiderate jerks I worked for, figuring out a way to legally not pay their contractors. Thankfully, I was going to be able to pay my bills the upcoming month, but I was not sure what to do after that. I decided I needed to take a break from life for a few days. I was going to care for my dogs, sleep and re-evaluate my life, once I had energy.

Chapter 21

Where God Guides God Provides

As the days progressed, I began to feel better. I really needed time alone with just my dogs. Once again, I had bitten off more than I could chew. I realized I needed to set stricter limits on what I could and could not do. I decided I was going to stop having house guests. I love my friends and family, but I needed my home to be calm. For close to four months my house was like a hotel with visitors from out of state. Everyone who came to my home helped out with my dogs, and I enjoyed having their company, but changing sheets for each visitor, house cleaning per visitor, and providing food was expensive. I was exhausted, and I needed a quiet home until I was in a better mood.

This decision weeded out my real friends, from ones who came for a free dip in the pool and food. The word *no,* coming out of my mouth was foreign to some of them and they did not like hearing it. I realized when I said "No, I am not hosting," or "No, I cannot afford that right now." A few people slipped out of my life. Learning I had a few fake friends did stink, but it was better to have them leave my life sooner versus later.

I evaluated how much time my dogs consumed, with different medications and dietary needs every morning and night. At that time, food prep alone took 30 minutes. Luna was ready for adoption, and I needed to change my dogs' schedule to tire Luna out, then put her away and let Logan out alone. I spent time promoting Luna on all social media platforms as well, trying to find her the perfect loving forever home.

I had to change my routine to protect Logan. Luna would stay with me while Logan and Lucy went outside. This made her sad. She loved play time and detested being separated from them. I know she thought I was being a miserable old lady, for not letting her play with her friends. I had spoiled Luna just as badly as I had Logan, while she was getting better. Therefore, she became a bit of a crybaby when she did not get her way. Her whimpers would get louder the longer as she waited for her turn in the yard. Logan would come in and go directly in his crate. Lucy would follow him and sit next to his crate to comfort him, she is an amazing mother.

Then Luna and I would play outside. I was thankful and happy that Luna was healed. In my heart, I felt Luna and Logan both deserved better. Logan was my dog, I felt terrible that Luna annoyed him, and sometimes she accidentally hurt him during his recovery. This was the most frustrating month I had with my dogs. I believed Luna would be happier being the only dog, constantly being the center of attention and being a family princess in another home. For a while Luna had been mad at me over her first adoption, I wondered if she would always hold a grudge toward me. She destroyed my living room furniture, even though I am not materialistic, not having a place to sit to watch TV added to how overwhelmed I was feeling.

The rescue and I knew that Luna was healthy enough to get a new home. Everyone agreed to promote her as many places as possible. I believed a new home for Luna would make everyone happier.

Once I figured out I needed to cut back on hosting, had a new schedule set up for my dogs, I was onto reviewing my finances. Again, there was no money coming into my home. The past year and a half had been a consistent financial struggle, the economy was awful. I was continually being told I was over-educated. I had received over 1,000 job rejections. The only work I could find was contractual. I did my best with my finance, but unexpected things happened, costing money. My air conditioner died and needed to be replaced, my car needed new tires, my laptop broke, and then my poor baby Logan needed a knee. Despite being extremely frugal, my emergency money was depleted. This is the scariest and most stressful feeling I have ever felt. I cannot put into words what the fear of losing my home and my having utilities shut off was like, but it sucked.

Once, I paid my bills for the month I had $30.30 left in my bank account. I was going to need to cut more cost. I only had internet, I never had cable for my TV, but the internet needed to go. I was fortunate, my phone had unlimited data. I am an active library, user so I went there to use the internet. I learned they had a good selection of movies to check out for entertainment too. Later a friend gave me a TV antenna, which gave me 19 channels. I went through my home and realized how many duplicates of things I had. I decided to have a giant yard sale. I posted the night before on all social media platforms and made over $400.00. What I could not get rid then, I sold to a pawn shop.

    Having fewer people in my home decreased my grocery bill. After the yard sale, I went food shopping with an overload of coupons. As I was picking up the ingredients to make the dog treats for the local farmers market, randomly I decided to buy all the ingredients and experiment with other recipes I had not yet tried. It would be great if I could sell them, but if I had to bring them home my dogs would eat them.

    Each day that week I experimented with a new dog treat recipe. I created new advertisements, sales, and promotions for the upcoming farmers market. I had a few friends text me that day wishing me good luck, words of encouragement and prayers. I was not the only one going through financial hard times, it was comforting to have so many people be understanding and supportive of what I was going through. My new table of new treats was a success. The market opened at 9:00 a.m. My treats sold out by 10:30 a.m. What was even better was a dog trainer decided to have class at the farmers market, right in front of my booth. I sent pictures to my friends and said, "Your prayers are working, a dog class is taking place right in front of my booth. The pet parents are buying all my products!"

    Vending at the farmers market was successful. I was going to be able to scrape by one more month. I was counting my blessings in between being completely confused as to how I got into such a state of living so scarcely. I thought I had done everything right to prevent this. It took me a very long time to figure out.

One day out of the blue my mother called me, she explained that I had inherited $6,000.00. Apparently, there had been items sold from an estate that had been forgotten about. The money was to be given to me. My stress was over for at least a couples months. I remember a friend said to me, "Melissa, although this is hard you are truly being guided to care for these dogs."

I was still discouraged and tired but felt more at ease having a financial cushion again. I acknowledge this was an answer to my prayers, but in the back of my mind I felt incomplete and lacking because I still did not have a *real* job.

Lessons Learned

The Importance of Self-Care

What I learned in a hard way is the importance of self-care and self-love. When I was honest with everyone that I was overwhelmed and needed to take a break I received a great deal of support. Friends sent me articles about caretakers who had reached their limit but kept a public façade that everything was okay. When I shared my exhaustion with people, the majority of my friends understood.

The word *no* comes out of my mouth a lot more than it used to. Through caring for my dogs, I learned more about my personal limits. Animal rescue is what I am meant to do. I am living out my calling. In order to effectively help each animal that walks into my home, I need to be physically and emotionally healthy too.

Saying *no* demonstrates self-love and self-respect. Those who cannot acknowledge that tend disappear. So it decreases superficial relationships. Let's be honest, no one really likes those affiliations anyway.

I know I am not alone in thinking I can do more than I actually can, at times. I would advise people that if they did not care for themselves, they could not help others. I needed to follow this advice myself. I had to learn the hard way exactly what my limits were.

The role of women in society has changed. We have gone from primary caretakers to caretakers, plus professionals at the majority of things we seek to try. Our expectations of ourselves have increased, and we have misconstrued the saying *you can have it all*! Yes, we can have it all, but having it all at once, and doing it all at once, is overwhelming and exhausting! The joy from the saying is completed robbed because of a *must have it all right now* mentality we have created.

I still struggle with this at times. I have changed my mindset to *today, I will do my best*. If I do not accomplish everything, I go to bed considering all the things I did accomplish, regardless of how small it is.

Vetting & Money Saving Tips

Before this, I sincerely defined myself as frugal, but I had to learned new strategies to save and stretch a dollar.

Veterinary Care – Medical for dogs is very costly. My dogs have their own vet who they visit when they are sick. They are all caught up on their shots, heartworm, and flea and tick medication as well. However, my dogs go to a local non-profit organization for shots, blood work, and their yearly heartworm test. This costs $50.00 per dog.

Today, many pet stores, local animal shelters, and mobile vetting trucks provide affordable shot for dogs and cats. This is important because it prevents them from getting rabies, parvo, canine distemper, influenza (the flu), and leptospirosis. Trust me when I tell you, many of these diseases are deadly and expensive to cure. More expensive than shots, and monthly supplements that prevent them.

Heartworm – Heartworm is a serious concern, and is prevalent in all 50 states. In 2017, it was reported that Florida and many other southern states had 700 new species of mosquitos arrive. The increased hurricanes and tropical storms carried these bugs in from other locations. Mosquito bites cause dogs to contract heartworm. This is a very painful disease, but curable. White string-like worms grow inside the valves of the dog's heart. As the worms grow they clog the valves and major blood vessels in the heart. This makes it difficult for the heart to properly function, damaging the dog's heart and impacting other major organs. If the heartworm is not treated the dog will die an excruciating and cruel death. Therefore, placing your dog on heartworm prevention is a must. There are several different heartworm medications available. Discuss with your vet which prevention method best fits your dogs need. There are tablets that are given once a month and some that last up to three months.

Medicine- Medication can become costly for animals and humans alike. Talk with your vet regarding what over the counter vitamins and human medications your pet can have. As I explained, I have my dogs on fish oil, glucosamine chondroitin, and bone broth for their collagen regrowth. I am an avid coupon cutter, online promo code user, and conduct online searches to find mobile coupons too. Most forms of heartworm prevention offer promotions and discounts to affordably protect your dog.

Additionally, some pharmacies offer specific antibiotics for $4.00 or less. I recommend looking online for what medications they specifically are and talk to your vet about having your dog or cat on the generic brands. Lastly, I recommend going to the stores that allow you to use multiple coupons on the same item, especially, when they are buy one get one free.

Let's all do our best to keep our furry family members healthy. They are family!

Chapter 22

Let's Go Luna-Let's GO!

On the days that I was not at a farmers market, job hunting or at the vet, I was at adoption events with Luna. I whole-heartily felt she would be better in another home being the only dog with more people around to praise her. I knew I was going to miss her. She had become a big part of my life. It is impossible to care and sacrifice for someone, without falling in love. At the same Luna was a challenging pup for me. Her destruction of my things was really upsetting. I did replace my living room furniture when I received my inheritance from a thrift store. The furniture is functional, but I did not want to buy anything that I was going to absolutely love because I was afraid it would get ruined. I was right about this as both Logan and Luna did nibble on the end of the new sofa when I wasn't looking.

Luna attended weekly adoption events. I met one family that I thought would be a perfect fit for her. Their daughter loved Luna and she was just as affection back. I really wanted them to adopt her, but they wanted to foster dogs instead, which naturally, I find admirable.

As I was talking to the woman, about Luna's good and bad traits, she interrupted me, and said, "You really love this dog!"

Until she said it to me, I did not realize just how much I did love Luna. I wanted to protect from ever being harmed again regardless of how crazy she could drive me.

The rescue arranged for Luna to be on TV. This was one of the greatest days of her life. She knew it was going to be all about her when I would take out her pink bandana. As soon as she sees it she runs toward it to have it put on. She then sits up straight to be brushed and have puppy perfume sprayed on her. She enjoys all this attention and pampering, she is a bit of a diva. When we got to the TV studio, Luna did not want the other dogs to be around and was acting out to protect me. Having a German Shepherd show all their teeth is scary, so I had to leave. I left her with my friend who was going to take her on the show and waited in the car. 30 minutes later Luna pranced out of the studio, prouder than I ever saw her prance before getting into my car. She was definitely pleased with what happened. My friend explained that Luna was a natural on screen. She sat still and smiled directly at the camera the entire time.

We went to my mom's house to watch Luna's first TV appearance which was going to air later in the morning. All my friends tuned in as well. Wow, Luna loved the attention. The people at the station even had a song that played in the background with the lyrics singing *Luna's coming home* before and at the end of the interview. We shared Luna's video throughout Florida to promote a new home for her. It was clear Luna loved every second of being on TV and being granted Tampa Bay's Dog of the Day title. I was asked a few times if Luna's head was able to fit through the door when she got back to my house, it was obvious Luna was impressed with herself.

Sadly, we still could not find the perfect home for her. I reached out to Roger who had fallen in love with Logan. Six weeks earlier his dog Trooper had passed away. The family was beginning to feel ready to adopt again. I told the rescue that if Roger wanted to adopt Luna, she would have a wonderful life. They okayed the visit. Luna and I spent four days with Roger and his family. We took Luna to the beach, the pet store to get toys, and countless car rides. Everyone cheered for Luna when she was able to lift herself up on the sofa all by herself. At night Luna slept with me but would leave the room if she heard someone else was up. She knew her cuteness would get her treats. They all loved Luna and had a family meeting about adopting her. Before I left with Luna, Roger's mother said to me, "Luna has found a home and it's amazing."

"Really," my face instantly lit up, "You want to adopt her? This is going to be her new home?"

"No, Melissa we cannot take Luna, she has a home with you. You have made your house a home for her."

"No, Luna doesn't like me. She tolerates me but is upset with me for the first home she went too. She wants something more than what I can give her." I said in a solemn tone.

"Give it time, Melissa, she knows she has it good with you, she has picked you, and that is why there are no other suitable homes for her, God has his hand in this."

I drove home disappointed that they did not want to adopt Luna. I noticed Luna was sleeping in the front of my car with a huge smile on her face. She had a fun vacation and got a few new toys. I had a great time with her and my friends. After the trip, Luna transitioned into the sweet, and well behaved pup I once knew. I realized she was appreciating all I was doing for her. Although I will never forget her destructive phase, that stage drove me nuts. I was thankful, the stress and annoyance of not knowing what trouble she was going to get herself into next finally ended. She would still sass anyone if she felt disrespected, and she enjoyed teasing other dogs, but overall, she was very loving.

When Luna had gotten spayed, she had a tough time walking afterward. She was confused and did not understand why her legs were giving out on her again. It took three days for her to be able to walk on her own. Looking back at that time, I had slept on the living room floor next to her, in a sleeping bag to comfort her, and ensure she would not hurt herself worse trying to walk. She was light enough to carry to and from the bathroom. I had become so adjusted to sitting on the floor caring for injured dogs, that sleeping on the floor for a few nights did not bother me. I was learning just how temporary these phases of life are.

I had adjusted my schedule to give Luna one-on-one time and manage everything else. Logan had his leg surgery six months ago. For six months Luna was out with me at least once a week trying to find the perfect home. Beside her short stay at the lousy home, I had Luna since she was eight weeks old and we were approaching her first birthday. I even had a surprise birthday party for Logan, Luna, and

Buddy. At this point, I acknowledged just how much I loved her. It was clear she was a happier pup. I knew the whole house was going to be different when she left.

Chapter 23

When you Gotta Go-You Gotta Go!

As summer of 2017, was coming to an end the past six months had been jam-packed with caring for Lucy and Chimayo. Helping Logan recover from his knee surgery, and taking Luna to countless adoption events. On top of that, I was committed to finding more contracts or a new job. I had a gotten a new professional haircut, power suit and business cards made. I even self-published some of my former research into books in hopes of impressing the right hiring manager. I attended numerous job fairs, networking events, and I lost count of how many interviews I had gone on. I had learned how to stretch, save and cut financial corners but I wanted the security of a weekly paycheck. There were days that I would fall asleep as soon as

I sat down. But this schedule came to an abrupt stop the first week of September.

Hurricane Irma, a category five hurricane, was expected to hit, and possibly desolate Florida. Words will never be able to explain, the emotions that went along with learning my home could be completely destroyed, but I will do my best. Floridians knew that we would be getting a hurricane, but that is what our state is known for. We even joke that we drink hurricanes, but there was something different about this storm that almost the entire state was being cautious of. Everyone seemed to experience an eerie feeling, warning us that Hurricane Irma was to be taken seriously.

On Monday night, I went to the store the stock up on food. We were told to have at least three weeks supply of water. I knew I needed more than that for my dogs. All the stores I went to had empty shelves. Almost everyone I spoke with was in fear. The storm was expected to hit on Sunday, six days away.

By Tuesday night, people started to evacuate, regardless of if the area they lived in needed to be evacuated or not. I was beginning to get scared. The news explained that if an area needed to be evacuated and the people refused to leave, the rescue crew would not help them. All I could think about was me trying to get Lucy on the roof while my home flooded with water. Then trying to get her to stay calm and hopefully have a helicopter rescue us. She still did not like to be touched; she scared easily and had become a bit of a fatty over the past year. Then I thought about how many days we would be sitting there, or even worse we would all die. I know it sounds morbid, but it was realistic.

    I spoke with my cousin who has a house in Georgia. He generously said my dogs and I were welcome to stay there during the storm. He invited my mother, her dogs and another cousin in Florida and her dogs. I was the only one who accepted his offer. The news explained that the weather reports would not be able to determine until 24 hours before the storm hit, which coast would be affected. If it was going to come up the Gulf of Mexico, Irma would directly hit Tampa Bay. Every time I heard the news reports chills went down my spine. After saying goodbye to three of my friends on Tuesday and speaking with others who had booked hotels out of state. I decided to accept my cousins' offer and evacuate sooner versus later.

    I went to the vet and got sleeping pills for my dogs. I suspected a very stressful trip, considering Chimayo does not like the pups, and Lucy has high anxiety. Yet, they also sensed something was off and were on their best behavior.

    Before leaving, I had a list of things I needed to complete, in hopes of keeping my house safe. It was the strangest feeling to drive through my neighborhood, watch us all pack our cars and trucks the best we could, and as fast as we could. I went to the hardware store to get the boards for my windows, doors, and garage. My neighbors rented a chainsaw, and many of us cut down our trees to prevent them from falling on one another's houses. I rented a sump pump to drain 3 ft. out of my mother's pool and mine. I purchased over-priced gas canteens to fill up for the trip. All outdoor furniture needed to be put inside our homes, this may sound simple, but it was a lot of work.

Everything seemed different before Hurricane Irma was approaching. Things that I had cared about before had lost importance. My neighborhood and beyond had gone into survival mode. There was no concern about work, meeting deadlines or making plans. We cared about being safe, if we made it back to our homes we wanted ours and everyone around us to be intact.

The hardest part about everything that was going on was my mother did not want to evacuate. She watched the news of the confusion on the highway, the traffic jams, and listened to other people who survived hurricanes their entire life. They had decided they were not going to leave this time either. My mother and I disagreed with me taking my dogs to my cousin's home, and imposing on him. For me, the risk of staying was too high.

My biggest fear was for Lucy. I knew with her anxiety if the storm hit Florida she would be the dog the rescue team may leave behind to save calmer ones. I made a promise to care for ALL the dogs under my roof, and if it meant leaving my home to keep them safe, then that is what I needed to do.

My goal was to hit the road Thursday afternoon, but getting my house hurricane safe took longer than anticipated. On my way to fill up the gas canisters, the radio sent out an emergency evacuation of my zone. Although I was leaving that evening, this put me in the weirdest state of panic I ever knew. I turned my car around and ran into my mother's house. I breathlessly came through the door and said, "I have to evacuate, PLEASE COME!"

My mother said it was too late for her to come with me. The drive would tire her out, and that her flood zone (.5 miles away from mine) did not get evacuated. She was trying to explain to me on the map that it was not my flood zone. She insisted the news report had made an error, but I did not care. The people who lived across the street from my house had a creek at the end of their property, deep enough for them to kayak in and for alligators to swim in. This fact and the radio announcement was enough for me to decide to leave. The hardest part of my evacuation was leaving my mother. Yet, she was determined to stay, in hopes the storm would hit the east coast of Florida.

Feeling defeated, I went and got my gas, and two energy drink to keep me awake through the nights' drive. I came home gave the dogs their sleeping pills and started to pack the car with their items. After I had packed for the dogs, I grabbed two backpacks and packed for myself. I opened each of my bureau drawers and pulled out the top three items. I was not sure what I was packing but did not care. My appearance and favorite clothing no longer mattered; keeping my household safe was now my number one concern.

Farewell my Friends

Once packed I said farewell to my neighbors this was a somber moment. We did not know what our future held for us anymore. Our daily routines may never be the same within the next 48 hours. There may not even be a neighborhood to return to. Would our next meeting be rummaging through piles of cinderblock and wood looking for items in what was once our home?

We hugged I exchanged phone numbers with neighbors I did not know before the hurricane. Over the next few days, we all kept in communication with one another. Notifying each other about detours, roadblocks, and news we heard about our homes.

It was 9:30 p.m., Thursday evening. I needed to be out of my neighborhood by 8:00 a.m. Friday morning. I put my four drugged dogs into my car, the sleeping pills had kicked in. Chimayo sat in the front seat next to me. Luna, Logan, and Lucy sat in the back on blankets and dog beds. I went to my mother's house one last time to say goodbye and drove away. In all honesty, if it was not for Lucy's high anxiety, I may have stayed, but in my heart, I believed it was best for everyone to if we evacuated. After all, it was mandatory.

For the first four hours, I was disgusted with the entire situation. I felt horrible leaving my mother, I wanted to throw up, but I was so busy over the past few days that I had little to eat. I had been too stressed to want to eat. My dogs behaved like perfect angels the entire trip to my cousins. On a regular day, it would take seven hours to get to his home, with everyone evacuating it took 16 long, boring and emotional hours. I knew I was fortunate for my cousin to allow my dogs and I to stay with him. In fact, I think it is one of the kindest things anyone has ever done for us. The stress was no longer seeing my future. I was safe, my dogs were safe, but would I have a home in 48 hours? Would my mother and her dogs be alive in 48 hours? I could only hope.

Chimayo slept the entire trip. The sleeping pills really hit him hard. Luna and Logan woke up eight hours later. They kept looking over the front seat at Chimayo. He usually growls at them and makes mean faces. They did not know what was that matter with him. Lucy woke up, I saw her start to stretch and move around in her bed. At first, she looked worried but while stretching noticed all the cars and traffic out the rear window. She sat right in the middle of the back seat amused and taken by all the activity she saw. She spent the entire trip either sleeping or people watching.

When we finally arrived at my cousins', I was exhausted. I let the pups out of the car. They instantly started running around. My cousin's yard is much bigger than mine. They had big smiles on their faces while running through the yard releasing all their pent-up energy. I took Lucy out of the back seat and tied her to my cousins railing in the yard. Then I got Chimayo out. My poor senior dog was very stiff from sitting so long, we both needed massages. Chimayo got a massage from me. I got one a few days later.

My cousin's house was set up perfectly for the dogs to be close to me and in their crates. Chimayo stayed in my room. Lucy, Luna, and Logan slept in the large bathroom attached to my bedroom. I had brought Lucy's favorite king size bed for her to sleep in. To this day I still laugh that I packed her oversize bed as one of the most essential items needed, but I did. Logan and Luna were crated. Once I was situated, I went to the thrift store to get the pups fluffy blankets to sleep on and a crate for Chimayo. When my phone was charged, I called everyone I knew to tell them we were safe, took a quick shower, and fell asleep within minutes of my head hitting the pillow. My cousin was arriving the next day.

Lucy's Home

I woke up rested the next morning. Although my dogs slept most of the car ride there, they understood I was exhausted, they kept quiet, and allowed me to sleep as long as I needed. When I did wake up, I felt refreshed. I took Logan, Luna, and Lucy outside on their leashes. The property was big, with no fence. I did not want them to wander and get lost. I hooked them up to the bottom of my cousin's giant trampoline. I went into the house and got my coffee, while I sat under a tree I stopped watching my dogs, and looked up at the giant oak tree with a cardinal singing in it. It was as if he was singing to me. He was a really bright red while looking down at me he was tapping is little foot. I was so entertained I did not realize Lucy had gotten off her leash and was no longer attached to the trampoline.

My mind went into full panic mode. I walked the property for close to 45 minutes, I could not find her. I took Logan and Luna inside the house. I was going to get into the car, and drive around the neighborhood to try and find her. Just as I finished putting Logan and Luna in their crates, I walked into the kitchen to see Lucy staring at me. I was so relieved, excitedly I said, "Lucy, you're back!"

She casually walked past me with a big smile on her face, while wagging her tail she went into the bathroom to lie down on her bed. After that, I realized I was able to open the door, let Lucy out to explore, and trusted she always came back. This confirmed that Lucy knew her home was with me. I understood that no matter where we were she would come back to me. She was happy being my very unique dog.

A Turn for the Worse

While Logan, Luna, and Lucy were sleeping, I took Chimayo with me to drive around the area. While driving to the local store, it came on the radio that the storm track was determined; Hurricane Irma was headed directly toward Tampa, FL. The news sent me into a panic. I pulled into the nearest shopping stripped and burst into tears. It had been the longest and most exhausting week I ever had. Chimayo sat in the back of the car watching me. I think every negative emotion was pouring out of me. I was tired, stressed, angry at my mother for not evacuating with me, and worried about friends who had to stay. I had begged my mother since Monday to leave with me, now on Saturday, the weather reports determined a category five hurricanes was headed straight toward my home.

While I sat in the parking lot sobbing my mother called. I could tell by the sound of her voice she was scared. She said that the neighbors that have lived in Florida their whole life and never evacuated were headed to the shelter. She did not have enough crates to take her dogs and felt trapped. My mother's fear must have been far worse than mine. As she was talking to me she started crying, she told me, she was proud I evacuated, that I was a hero to my dogs and apologized for giving me a hard time about it. As she was saying this to me, we got disconnected.

I cried in my car even more, I tried to pull myself together so I could turn that car around and drive back to my cousins. When I finally calmed down, I went to the local store instead. The parking lot was full of Florida cars. The store must have made a significant profit that week. Most customers' were evacuees needing basic supplies they forgot to pack. I needed a toothbrush. While shopping I bumped into a woman. She told me her daughter worked for the local news station in Tampa. They were recommended to evacuate as early as possible because they were predicting it was going to be the worst storm the United States ever had. This made me sick to my stomach. I got my toothbrush and went to my car. I started to cry again I posted on social media what they lady told me, hoping it was not too late for more friends to evacuate.

While I was crying my mother called. She was calm, and explained she was going to stay with friends who lived inland. They told her to bring her dogs. They did not seem too worried about the storm from their location. This put my mom at ease. I felt better knowing she was not going to go through the storm alone. She explained she needed to gather her things and would call me later that day, before the electricity would be out.

When I got off the phone, I cried yet again, this time it was cries of relief. My mom was at ease and hopefully would be safe. I went into the store again, washed my face and tried to look a bit presentable for my cousin's arrival. All the way back to my cousin's home I prayed. I asked God to keep every person and animal left in Florida safe. I am sure I prayed more during the two weeks of Hurricane Irma than I had my entire life. I believe every Floridian did.

I arrived back at my cousin's house the same time he did. I met his girlfriend for the first time. They were amazing hosts. They did everything they could to keep my mind off what was going on in Florida. My cousin loved Chimayo. Chimayo loved being considered the number one dog too. He was having a great time. My cousin's girlfriend and Lucy bonded. I was excited to see this. Although, I was more stressed than I have ever been Lucy was relaxed and enjoying herself. Watching my dogs have fun on my cousin's 5 acres, took my mind off everything else going on. They gave me something to laugh about.

Within 24 hours I was able to let all the dogs out in his yard to play without a leash. They ran around having a great time. It was as if they knew where my cousin's property ended and did not want to go any further. As I sat in the backyard watching them, I knew if I needed to relocate my dogs, we would be very happy to find our own home in this small town.

Bye-Bye Bayshore

When my dogs were settled, I would watch the news. All the water was pulled in from the bay almost 200 miles. At this point I was numb. I was too tired to be stressed. I prayed silently while I helped put together my cousins' new bookshelf to distract me from what was going on back home. Over the evening the water returned to the bay in a very calm manner. When the water was retracting the weather reports predicted the storm could turn into a tsunami. Fortunately, for Floridians, we were spared of this natural disaster, but other parts of the state were not as fortunate. My neighborhood only lost electricity a few days later while the state was working to get electricity back to everyone.

I spoke with friends who could not evacuate. They explained sitting in their homes hearing the raging storm outside was the scariest thing they ever went through. They felt like sitting ducks, acknowledging that at any moment they could have the roof ripped off their home or be flattened while they were inside. When they share how they felt about hearing the storm all around their homes, their eyes are wide, and you can see the fear in their faces. The city officials of Tampa, Fl., declared the water calmly returning into the bay was a miracle.

A Homecoming

I stayed at my cousin's home for one week. The storm had knocked down trees, and some of the state did not have gasoline. If I returned too early, it would be another 16 hour car ride. I was not sure I had the energy to make that drive again.

The week became an evacuation vacation. I took my dogs on the local trails, and parks in the area. I realized how much I enjoyed being able to have them with me while I explored. The time away was revitalizing. Each day I explored a new location and made memories with my best friends. Logan was so excited that he would run to the edge of the property, he would then start to dance, and spin in circles until he fell over smiling. Luna had an extra bounce to her step, Lucy smiled more than I had ever seen, and Chimayo loved my cousin introducing him as the coolest dog.

The evening before I left I did my best to clean my cousin's home. He likes dogs, but with his work schedule does not have any. I understood my fours dogs, although behaved were a bit overwhelming to him. I decided I was going to leave at 3:00 a.m. to avoid Atlanta, GA rush hour traffic, and get home as early as possible. This worked once the house was clean, I went to bed. I got up at 2:30 a.m. to give the dogs their sleeping pills. Let them out to go to the bathroom, packed the car, and headed home to Florida. To stay awake, I had bought another two energy drinks the night before.

The ride home was smooth. It took less than seven hours. Schools were back in session, so the worst of the traffic was over. Friends called me to see how my trip was going. My dogs were so well behaved some asked if I had brought them home. One friend said, "I have been checking on all my friends, your car is the quietest, do you really have four dogs?"

I looked at all my dogs; Lucy was sitting in her bed smiling. I realized she understood she had a family, she finally acknowledged she was loved just as much as the other dogs. Lucy understands she is different, I know she would like to trust a person to pet her, but she is not ready. That does not matter to me, she is my dog, and I love her the way she is. Lucy was the key reason I evacuated. I was scared I would be forced to leave her if I needed to be rescued myself. I would not be able to live with that guilt and regret. The bond between Lucy and I was tighter than ever. She acknowledged and appreciated just how much I loved her.

We arrived home before noon. Before going to my house, I went to see my mom. Logan and Luna were awake by then, and hanging their heads out the window. My mom came outside to greet us. Chimayo remained sound asleep in the front seat, the sleeping pill really hit my senior dog hard. I gave my mother a huge hug and told her I was going home to rest. I was not sure if I would see her again later that day.

My neighborhood was in the process of being fixed up. There were a lot of tree branches, leaves and debris to be cleaned up, but everyone I saw was smiling. It was the realization that we were fortunate to have a yard and house to clean up. It would take a couple weeks, but the yards and outdoor exterior of our homes would be repaired. Everyone acknowledged the city of Tampa received a miracle, spared from a category five hurricane and a possible tsunami.

I pulled into my garage, got my dogs and their things out of the car. I went to bed with a heart full of gratitude. Little did I realize then just how much I was going to need this spirit of appreciation in the days to come.

Driving back to Tampa, Lucy sitting on her king size bed

Chapter 24

The Road to Recovery

The next week after Irma still felt as if the real world no longer existed. While at my cousin's house I had emailed and sent out thank you cards for the companies that had interviewed me prior to Florida going into a State of Emergency. Sadly, some parts of Florida were drastically affected by Irma. The storm impacted businesses located in multiple locations. As I was focused on getting my house back in order, cleaning my front and backyard, I knew in the back of my mind my money was running low again.

By the end of the week, I received rejections letters and emails from all the companies I had interviewed with. Some businesses explained that they needed to implement a hiring freeze because of the damage that was done to their buildings in other parts of Florida. Other letters said they decided to hire another candidate. I was so frustrated and sick of being rejected. Once again I was broke!

In my mind, I had done everything right. I went to college, earned the highest possible degree for business I could, I had written textbooks. I was the very first researcher allowed into areas to meet people that never did interviews. Why was this happening to me? Why did no one want to work with me anymore? Why? Why? Why? Why me? What did I do that was so horrible that no one wanted to work with me?

I could not even get a job working at the mall over the holidays. I had done that for years to save money on my business attire. I felt like the whole world was against me and it sucked. As I was sitting at my table feeling sorry for myself my friend Kayla called. We had committed to helping one another with repairs in our home to save money. Plus we would get to see one another. She could tell I was defeated by the sound of my voice. I told her the mail from the past three weeks had arrived, I had a pile of new rejections letters, and very little money left. In a calm voice, she said, "Have you considered dog walking and pet sitting? There are a few places to advertise your services, and with your dog experience you should get customers easily?"

I was dumb-founded, "No, I never considered that, but I will."

This was just a perfect suggestion and job fit. Why didn't I think of it! For over two years I had been spending my money sending out applications. Kayla explained that some of our other friends set up profiles on different websites and started to get pet-sitting jobs fairly quickly. Later that week our mutual friend Denise came to help clean up my backyard from Irma. When we were finished, she sat with me and showed what websites she was using to advertise her services. Within five days of completing all the profiles, people started to contact me needing care for their dogs.

It was fall, so I filled out applications to return to vending my dog and cat products for the holiday season. All the places that I submitted my vendor application to responded with a cheery *Welcome Back* email.

You Own a Business - Silly

As I reflected on what was going on in my life, since getting laid off in July of 2015. I realized every time I applied to a teaching or research position regardless of how hopeful or positive the interviews went something would fall through. I came to the conclusion I needed to put 100% of my energy into promoting Love from Luke. I had hit financial rock bottom again. I took a half-hearted leap of faith when I wrote my first dog rescue book and started vending. I kept looking back at my past life thinking it was better than my present situation.

I understood I had started something with Love from Luke, but I needed to figure out exactly what I was doing. I can never say it enough about how blessed I am to have remarkably supportive friends. I had two friends who had started dog walking and pet sitting advertise my services as well. They sincerely wanted me to succeed. There were no concerns over competition or sharing their customers with me. Another friend gave me the gift of meeting with a business coach.

The business coach told me to bring some of my information and questions I had. My first question to her was, "Why can't I get a job? I have always been able to find work? I just don't get it!"

She looked at me a bit confused, and said, "Melissa, it is clear to everyone that you are in contact with, that you're an exceptionally smart and talented woman. You do not understand, but you started your own business on educating people on how to work with previously abused dogs. The people who interview you are waiting for you to see the entrepreneur spirit you exude."

The next thing she said to me really stuck. In an authoritative voice, she said, "Never expect to receive a paycheck from someone again. Expect to make larger paychecks with what you created with your dogs."

I was silent and stared at her wide-eyed. She then said, "Have you considered dog walking while you grow other aspects of Love from Luke?" I am sure my jaw just dropped as if I was collecting flies, this was the fourth recommendation for dog walking.

The business coach then asked questions about my first rescue book, this naturally led to me taking out my phone like a proud dog mom, show her my photos, and tell her all about Chimayo, Lucy, Luna, and Logan. I explained how my dogs are told they are blessed to be a blessing to others. As she learned about my dogs and my desire to get Luna and Logan into training to visit hospitals she blurted out, "You have a dog rescue! You have your own charity going on in your home. Dogs are expensive and with four dogs with medical needs, I am sure you give more to your dogs than you do yourself. I am going to give you instructions on what to do to become a non-profit and provide services to your community."

She went to her room to get the instructions on how to properly complete the required forms. She was excited about my goals. She was telling me about her own dog, and that she planned on purchasing my dog treats and book. My head was spinning, I was finally being given the direction and guidance I needed. The business coach was just as enthusiastic as I was about Love from Luke becoming a non-profit, as I was. When my session ended, I left with the same level of confidence and focus I had when pursuing previous goals that I had reached. I had direction, a clearer vision, and an understanding of the work I needed to do to create the dog rescue and sanctuary I wanted since my childhood.

Chapter 25

That was Then, This is Now!

I look back and marvel at how much my life has changed since the first time I hugged Luke. My horribly stinky and very dirty 95-pound Siberian Husky. I have written underneath my business cards *Angels come into our lives in all shapes, sizes and forms.* I believe this with all my heart.

When I was 23 years old, part of my job was to teach attorney's how to use new computer programs. I learned that I loved teaching and I was good at it. One of my goals was to become a college professor and teach adult learners. I have always enjoyed seeing individuals' faces light up from learning something new. I became a college instructor eight years later. I remember being in my early 20's, talking to my co-workers in the elevator on the way to work, expressing how much I enjoyed training adults.

As often as I said I wanted to teach, I also said I wanted to work full time with dogs. I remember telling friends and co-workers that someday I was going to have a store that sold pet products. I was going to help train dogs too. I wanted to achieve both these goals, and the desires to attain them were equally important to me. I even wrote both these goals down in a professional journal I kept. I would review the diary every six months or so to check off what goal was attained and then add a new one to the list. In my head I even imagined my store and rescue being in a beach or tourist type town. I remember thinking it was going to be in Maine and find it humorous that it started in Sunny Florida instead where it is usually beach weather year round.

My long-term goal is to have an animal rescue with lots of land in a scenic location (I really want the dog rescue building to be a log cabin, they are my favorite). My desire is to walk into a pound and pull all the animals off death row. Bring them to a supportive team who loves them and will help them to heal both medically and emotionally. When a dog is healthy, we will find them the loving forever home they have always dreamed of having. Every time one animal finds a home, I will help another.

Yet, in my mind my goal to work with rescued animals was when I retired from a very successful corporate job. I saw myself being older when my animal rescue started. When the doors began closing on research and teaching positions, I stood in front of the invisible door pounding on it, kicking it and full body slamming myself into it, insisting it re-open for me. All the while I unknowingly had created a store with my first Love from Luke book, unique pet jewelry, fresh baked vegan dog treats and countless other crafts I made and sold.

Looking back, I understand I let other's negative opinions of what I was doing with Love from Luke impact me. I allowed the few that stated my dog rescue, writing, and the pop-up store was a cute hobby, but not a respectable "real job." I gave these words too much authority over my goals versus listening to my intuition and heart's desire.

Returning back to Tampa after Hurricane Irma, with very little money left was my wake up call. I had manifested my biggest personal fear into reality. At this point, I was finally able to accept my new life and create the animal rescue I talked about since I was a child. I wholeheartedly accepted the work I was doing with special needs dogs was *exactly what I was supposed to be doing*. I took time and reflected on the events leading up to this. Everything that I attempted with Love from Luke; the promotion of the first book, vending, learning recipes for dog treats, applying as a vendor to local events and reaching out to various rescues in the Tampa Bay and surrounding area, I always received an excited, "Yes, we would love to work with you," response.

Once I finally acknowledged all the signs that I was supposed to do full-time rescue, I read one of Paulo Coelho books. I did not seek out his book, but found it in a waiting room at an appointment I had. In the *Notes from the Author*, he explained how he had a successful career, yet in the back of his mind he wanted to write books, but that was not deemed a practical choice. Why would anyone leave a promised paycheck, plus bonuses for a personal passion that may or may not succeed?

One morning he received a call that the company was letting him go. There were no warning signs, losing his job completely caught him off guard. Similar to my story, he searched for new employment for over two years, only to receive rejection after rejection. While he was looking for work, he would write in the evening. He had his book published, and over time it became an international bestseller.

What I related to most in Coelho's personal story was how he felt condemned by a cruel God who stopped hearing his prayers. Over time he realized God was leading him to his true calling in life. That each rejection was a lesson, he acknowledged that as soon as he felt he had mastered a situation something would happen to keep him grounded and humble.

Lastly, he explained that the pain and suffering he felt during his transition was to assist him in being attentive to the signs God had been sending him, while he was busy looking in the wrong direction. Coelho story gave me confidence in my struggles. His introduction decreased my sense of confusion and feeling lost. It provided new insight on my own career frustrations.

GOD spoke, I didn't Listen

I know God's timing is perfect, but I couldn't help thinking, why did I have to go through two-plus years of self-torture and interview mishaps before my friends started making recommendations to me? Was I so headstrong and determined to return to a corporate setting that I would not listen?

I clearly listened and believed the negative comments I received. That what I started with my dogs was cute, but had too much control over my life. I never realized that what I started with my four dogs was my life's calling. It was the reason I had so much joy while caring for them about 90% percent of the time, I was pursuing my truest passion.

I made returning to teaching and research was my key focus. I really loved teaching and researching so returning to the field would have satisfied me. I was able to find creativity and art in the business realm. I enjoyed formulating strategies, and having back up plan A, B and C. I liked having my ideas become a reality. But in all honesty, before my layoff, I was sitting behind my computer crying because of all the work that was dumped on me as they let other departments go. Leadership and students had become cruel under the stressful circumstances, and I dreaded turning on my computer to read my emails. Plus, each year the company cut expenses, my paycheck was decreasing while my workload increased. I then interviewed for jobs with no excitement about obtaining the professional title.

I never quit on a goal I had, but it took me another eight months to come to the revelation that I was job hunting because I was expected too. I openly admitted to friends I wanted a paycheck to invest in helping more animals. I was fortunate to have reached all the corporate and teaching goals I had wanted to at a young age. I had no real desire to work for someone else. But out of belief in the *normal life,* I kept applying, networking and interviewing. It took me over two years to understand that God's rejection was actually his redirection.

As many times as I had negative comments made to me about finding a job and working for someone else, I had even more people tell me that I was going to have to figure out how to work for myself. I blindly did not want to accept what they were telling me at that time.

I recognized that while I was busying myself with trying to find a real job. All my needs and wants were being met. I wanted for nothing, but I was too blind to acknowledge just how fortunate I was. I had witnessed miracles, received gifts of money, and healings for my dogs. I wondered if the heavenly realm was smiling when I finally caught on.

There are days I look back at my other life, having a consistent paycheck and knowing where it was coming from, but my path is different now. When I start to look back at my life and think it was better before, I always see a picture or a quote reminding me, *Don't look back you're not going that way!*

One time my friend was helping me photoshop some pet pictures. I got an alert on my phone for a corporate training job. As I was about to pull up the website, my friend turned my laptop off. Confused I looked at her, she laughed and politely said, "Melissa, dogs are your future!"

I smiled and nodded (feeling a little foolish) and returned to graciously being helped with a pet rescue project.

Chapter 26

Love from Luke Dog Sanctuary

As the months progress, my meeting with the business coach really had me motivated. I had been pursuing my passion, without realizing it. When I returned home from visiting my friend, I started to complete the paperwork to become a 5013c. I contacted a few people for guidance and advice to fill the forms out correctly the first time. Everyone I reached out was excited and willing to offer feedback and valuable advice. I was told and expected that the process would be long, that I would probably have to resubmit documents and paperwork more than once. But I was also encouraged to keep going because this goal could be achieved.

Much to my surprise about six weeks after I completed the forms and right before Christmas, I received a government letter stating *Congratulations you are officially Love from Luke Dog Sanctuary & Rescue!*

I was so ecstatic, I started jumping up and down, screeching happy sounds in my kitchen. Logan and Luna joined in, they were not sure exactly what I was doing, but dancing around in a fool manner looked like fun to them. Luna added in with some cheerful barks. Chimayo contributed with annoyed barks, he does not like the pup to get too excited in the house. My Lucy slowly wagged her tail with caution, while watching Logan, Luna and I with a concerned look on her face.

I quickly got into my car and drove to my mother's house. She was hosting more family members, and I wanted to share my good news, but my excitement was quickly deflated. I came into the house with a huge smile on my face and excitedly said, "Guess what?"

"What?" my mother said

"I was approved as a non-profit dog sanctuary; I have officially become Love from Luke Dog Sanctuary!"

My family members slumped back down in their chairs, with frowns on their faces. One said in a disappointed voice, "Oh, I thought you were going to tell me you had a job and we were going to pop open some champagne to celebrate."

Naturally, my face dropped to, no one was excited for me. This was a difficult task that I accomplished. Everyone who helped said it would take a couple of tries to complete the forms correctly before getting approved. I got the authorization letter on my first attempt, it was a big deal. My enthusiasm over this achievement was instantly robbed from me. I was angry and disappointed all at the same time. My family continued to tell me how hard the taxes would be and all the new challenges I had taken on. Finally, I told them to stop, I reminded them of all the other hard goals I had previously achieved, but they doubted that I could do this. I had enough, in a frustrated voice I said, "I am leaving!" and walked out of the house.

Keep Going, Regardless

I understood, it was best to discuss my goals about Love from Luke Dog Sanctuary with people who were self-starters, visionaries, and entrepreneurs. Otherwise, it led to feelings of disappointment, anger and fear of failing. I had to focus on the friends reminding me that I could do this! I had to review the checklist of what I had already achieved with my animals. I had to remind myself of all the prayers that had been answered for my animals, plus my own needs. I had to be thankful for my friends who did celebrate my new life and successes with me.

I had to be thankful for all the other things my family did do while I was in my career transition. A few family members did help with my bills. I appreciated and accepted the help, but I was humiliated that I needed assistance at my age. My mother would purchase items in bulk at the store and split what she got with me. All basic necessities were met. Plus, she helped me vend at farmers markets. I know this was a lot for her. Sitting in the hot Florida sun tires most people out. Yet, she remained a solid support, getting up at 6:00 a.m. every weekend to help promote my Love from Luke products. Over the holidays, my mother would go to both Saturday and Sunday events, then on Monday she would volunteer to help others. Despite my mother's concerns over my new ventures, her heart is in the right place and I am thankful for the support she has shown.

Since losing my job in 2015, many of my friends had started their own businesses. They had either gained success from their start-up or were on their way to attaining it. Their encouragement toward my new vision prevented me from getting discouraged and gave me hope. As the saying goes, "Tell me who your friends are, and I tell you who you are."

Looking back, I started my dog sanctuary the very day I got down on my knees, opened my arms wide with my head facing the ground and asked a 95-pound stinky husky to come to me. Without comprehending it at the time, that was the day I surrendered my old life and embraced my new life of helping animals. Personally, I love the fact that I started my new journey on my knees, my head bowed facing the ground, with my arms wide open. It is as if I was surrendering my old life to God, to learn my true purpose.

Later in a time of self-reflection, I realized, I independently became active in animal rescue within three weeks of moving into my neighborhood. There were too many cats getting themselves into trouble. One cat broke my front window, and another gave Chimayo a bad scratch in his eye. I was very upset about Chimayo getting hurt, and vet bills can get expensive. Fixing my window was also costly; it was from the 1970's and needed to be custom made, ugh!

To prevent further ruckus, I researched local rescues that allowed people to rent cat traps. I learned to cover the trap with a towel, but to keep the entrance open, then fill the trap with smelly food (sardines for example) to attract the cat. When the cat goes in the cage to get the food the door shuts behind them. Every Friday, I would go to the local rescue and rent as many cat traps as I could. Sunday night, I would trap the cats, on Monday morning, at 6:00 a.m., I would take the cats to the affordable clinic to get them fixed and their first sets of shots. Monday evening, I would pick the cats up, allow them to heal in my garage and then let them back into the neighborhood. I had a few neighbors who fed them. I did not talk too much about fixing the cats. I just did it for their well-being. After helping so many cats, I helped Luke, after Luke I continued to foster dogs.

I finally understood I was living exactly where I was supposed to, as if it had been divinely planned by God. I remembered when I purchased my home, how the woman at the closing said, "You are the first loan I have seen get approved in 6 months. Every closing I have had this year has been a full cash offer. You must be doing something to get this house."

I do not catch on as quickly as I should sometimes, but I am learning and doing my best. I am open to my friend's advice and guidance. In all honesty, I do not always know who will hire me to care for the animals or how vending at events will go. Yet, the needs of my dogs and my needs continue to be met. I learned it is okay to ask for help, to receive and accept what others want to give my dogs or to me. They are doing this out of love. When a person gives, they also receive joy. I am more gracious and appreciative of everything as well.

Lessons Learned

Through my time with Chimayo, Lucy, Logan, Luna and the other pups who have come in and out of my home, I had a career and spiritual transformation. I learned:
- That change although positive can be hard and daunting. At times more sacrificial than I ever realized.

- There is no such thing as being perfect. Trying to be perfect or appear like you have it all together is draining.
- I am still learning not to bite off more than I chew, to show myself love and care. This one I do struggle with at times.
- I am learning to admit my faults and shortcomings. That it is okay to say "No!"
- I learned to listen and accept positive feedback and suggestions. I have learned to listen and silently reject negative comments, and opinions that do not align with my goals.
- I count my blessings daily. I remind myself of all the things that did go right in a day and all the things I did complete.
- After Hurricane Irma, facing the reality that my house and all the items inside could be lost forever, I understand that things are just things. They can bring temporary happiness, but possessions are not permanent in life. New homes, new cars, and items purchased will depreciate and lose value. I am grateful and thankful for them but understand happiness is not found in things. I appreciate my cute little home, it has allowed me to help more animals than I can count. My new goal is for a larger home, and volunteers to help more animals in need.
- Show gratitude and appreciation to the ones who support you. Listen and be respectful to the ones that don't, but do not allow them to crush your goals. Show them the respect you wish they would show you.

- Doing what you love is amazing and scary all at the same time. Regardless of people saying failing is learning, those times flat out suck.
- Make Lists: Lists of what you need to get done, even if it's a small task, being able to check something off on a stressful day can provide great satisfaction. Review your list weekly to monthly to measure how productive you are. Wow, my college professor days, came out on this piece of advice!
- With any goal or project one seeks, it takes a community. Find your desired village via local networking, social media group, churches, and community centers. Seek them out and share your goals with them. United it can happen faster and be more enjoyable.
- There is no such thing as a small gift or donation.

Being an entrepreneur is not easy. In the beginning, there is constant hustle to get your next paycheck. There are countless books focused on how to successfully start your own business. Although I have founded a non-profit dog sanctuary, the same amount of work is required. The advice I can personally offer is: *stay humble, stay thankful, and pray consistently.*

I often tell people that when I hit my version of rock bottom, I twisted my neck and landed with my face sideways on a rock because I was so busy reminiscing about my past career. I enjoyed the majority of that life. I loved watching my students faces light up when they grasped something new. Having them laugh during group activities and speak highly of my class, confirmed at that time, I was doing precisely what I was supposed to. I was right where God wanted me to be.

Today, seeing an abused dog smile and wag their tails for the first time is what I am supposed to be doing. It's scary and hard sometimes, but the more I say, here is my problem God please help, the less stressful my new life is becoming. I am thankful that I have had so many self-realizations and I have changed so much over the past few years. I am definitely not the person I was when I first met Luke. My life is not where I thought it would be at age 42. I am happier than I could have ever imagined. I have accepted that I have very little control over things in life. This understanding is a big deal considering how Type A I used to be. I see a vast amount of senseless cruelty that humans have brought upon animals daily and to stay focused on emotionally healing the dog in front of me, I need an outlet of my own. I have this with writing (clearly), art projects and exercise.

Chapter 27

Life Today

Why do your Dogs Exist?

One day I went on a hike with one of my friends. My mom's dog Buddy had just gotten out of the hospital because he pulled muscles overplaying. I wanted to do something special with him. While we were walking I was asked, "Do you ever wonder why God made your dogs disabled? Do you ever wonder why they exist?"

It was a good question, I had never thought about it. I just accepted these were my dogs. I knew God had a hand in it because I had four special needs dogs, and I would help my mother with Buddy. Sometimes, I had five dogs that required my care. Until I had the question directly asked to me, I never considered why?

My first response was, "I love them. I fell in love with them first. Then learned they required extra care, I loved them too much to turn my back on them. I do not care that they are sick or different. I am not sure why they are with me, but I know there is a reason."

This was the second time I was asked this. When Logan was a year old, before Dr. Charlie shared some test results with me, he said, "Are you sure you want to keep this dog? Can you give him back to the rescue?"

I stood there and said, "No, Logan is my dog, HE IS MY DOG, I LOVE HIM, HE IS STAYING WITH ME." I kept repeating this. I was surprised I was being asked this question. I never quit with Luke. I never imagined giving up on Logan.

Dr. Charlie stopped my rambling and said, "Okay, I just want to prepare you that you are in for a ride with this dog and it may not always be easy."

I nodded my head and listened to Logan's medical report. But I saw miracles with so many of my dogs, the bad news no longer phased me.

My friend's question was now the second time I was asked about caring for special needs dogs. I realized this was going to be a question many people had. Not everyone understands what I am doing, but that's okay.

I explained that my dogs do not know they are unique. In their mind, they were normal dogs who do the same task a little differently. This is the same for children who are born with physical differences. They do not know they are unique until they are told by society. There are many amazing videos of children born without arms or legs who have taught themselves within the first year of their life how to do the same as a child born with arms, legs, 10 fingers, and 10 toes. These videos are inspiring.

Later in the evening when I was unwinding from the day the answer was given to me as to why my dogs exist. My dogs exist to teach others about compassion and encouragement. I sent my friend a text explaining my revelation, he texted me back "Good answer, I get it, I agree, I like it!"

Now that my dogs attend more rescue events I explain to people that my dogs are considered the lucky ones. When they are introduced, kind individuals who love animals tend to comment, "Oh, that poor baby."

I quickly stop my dogs from receiving pity. I explain they are clueless as to why someone would feel bad for them. There are far too many dogs that do need to experience and know what true love is. My dogs have their emotional and physical needs met, in the animal rescue world, they are winning at life. Last time Luna and Logan went to the vet, I was informed they are both very spoiled and I'm okay with that.

Furever Home

Once I became a dog sanctuary and was able to afford all vet bills for Luna, Lucy, Logan, and Chimayo, I spoke with the rescue and officially adopt Luna and Lucy. Lucy blossomed after evacuating with her during Irma. Taking Luna to various adoption events formed a strong bond between her and I too. She was with me for over 18 months, I could no longer imagine my life without them. I call Luna my surprise blessing. My friend John likes to remind me, she realized I needed her, personally, I think it's mutual. Lucy has done an excellent job of picking up where Luke left off with life lessons.

Chimayo

Chimayo is now 14 years old. He has been with me through the most significant events in my life. He is my best friend, and I love having him by my side. He is a very healthy senior dog, but I do acknowledge he is getting old. We play and go for walks daily. I no longer travel more than three days because I want to be close just in case something were to happen to him. I want be able to get back to him within a few hours. I recently decided to do something special just with Chimayo every day. I know that my time with him is limited and just like Luke, I do not want to have any regrets. I want to look back at my time with him and say, "Yes, we did it all!"

Lucy

Lucy is a remarkable dog. I love watching her become more confident and happy every day. She has accepted my house as her home, and knows she is part of a family. She enjoys car rides and trusts I will never abandon her. At Lucy's last vet visit she pranced out of the office, wagging her tail and smiling. Her body language shouted I am proud of my life and how far I have come. When I opened the car door, she jumped right in and grinned from ear to ear the entire ride home.

Sometimes when I am on the phone with a close friend, and they ask how Lucy is, I loudly brag about her so she can hear. I will catch her smiling while she peaks in at me from another room. I then turn and look directly at her, she can make and hold eye contact longer now. I frequently tell her how I wanted her to be my dog so badly that I lost sleep thinking about her. When I learned that she was going to be my dog, I was so happy because she has such a beautiful and gentle soul. As I say these kind words, Lucy wags her tail and smiles. She walks through the house for a couple hours with a silly grin on her face that I absolutely love!

I can only pet Lucy when she is afraid, but I love her as much as every dog that has entered my home. Lucy has taught me a great deal about being patient. She has demonstrated the impact of what being kind and gentle can create.

Luna

Luna is now two years old. I call her my surprise blessing and nicknamed her my Luna- Lunatic. When we a goofing off, I will sing a silly song for her to prance and dance to. What is even funnier is how much Lucy likes watching us be silly. I really think Lucy is laughing the entire time she smiles wide and wags her tail. Our ridiculousness delights her.

Luna has grown up to be my sweetest and most obedient dog. She listens to everything I say, and if she does not understand what I want her to do, she tries her hardest to figure it out because she wants to please me. In fact, she has gone from being one of my most destructive dogs to one of the most well behaved dogs I have had. She is the best listener out of the four. I am really thankful her chewing phase has passed. I try not to be materialistic, but I was pretty miffed when I had to get rid of my comfy sofa, then had to wait a few weeks to find a replacement. Sitting on my ottoman because my mischievous dog ruined the couch did frustrate me.

Luna will be attending dog training classes soon so she will be able to visit children in the hospitals. I already know she is going to strive in this environment; she loves being the center of attention. Luna can really work a crowd. She is a little bit of a diva. When Luna is going to go someplace special, she wears a pink bandana. I as soon as I show her the bandana she comes running and sticks her head through the loop I made. Once it is on, she lifts all her paws to be brushed and sprayed with puppy perfume. When it is cold she wears a dress and then she really prances to her destination. People instantly get a smile on their face when they see her proudly strutting down the street all dressed up.

Luna first has to learn to be tolerant of other dogs. Ever since her brief stay with the other family, she does not want any other dogs but my dogs around her. This issue will get resolved, it may take time, but it can be overcome. Luna and Lucy have surprisingly become very best friends. This happened when Logan was recovering from his surgery. Both Lucy and Luna preferred spending time with Logan, but he could not run around while healing. One day Luna initiated play with Lucy and instantly Lucy responded running around as playful and as youthful as Luna. When Lucy is tired, Luna smiles, kisses her face and lies down next to her. They have come a long way from tolerating and making snarling faces at one another.

Luna will always be on a high vitamin diet and requires check-ups to ensure her spine and legs keep working. Luna IS a miracle, she loves and is loved by many. I am so thankful I have been able to watch Luna physically heal and become such a sweet, kind and fun-loving dog.

Logan

Logan is doing amazing. He has the brightest sweetest smile and is always happy. He is my 90-pound gentle giant, my special gift from God, reminding me to never stop helping animals or give up on the animals deemed hopeless or unwanted. I have to confess, I do baby him more than the other dogs. I am always concerned he will overdue and hurt his leg. I am a helicopter pet parent with him, and he can act spoiled at times.

Logan is currently on a high collagen, fish based diet. I have all of my dogs on a high dosage of glucosamine, with MSM and vitamin D. I also give them steamed kale and sweet potatoes. This is easier than it sounds. I toss the food into a crockpot and go about my day. Watching Logan run and play with Lucy and Luna is a good sign that it is working. Logan loves to play hide and seek with Luna, but he likes to be the one who hides and the one that gets chased. He is the first to come in from play and sit right next to me to watch whatever I am doing. Sometimes he will sleep right outside my bedroom door, snoring (the same place Luke slept). He will also cry for me to come out of my bedroom and pet him if he feels we need to spend more time together. Another thing Luke used to do.

Logan comes with me to farmer markets, dog rescue events or to check out other things to do in the community. As do all my dogs, they love getting to be the only dog, meeting new people and getting all the attention. Logan especially likes going to the adoption events. Most of these events Logan relaxes in a crate with a fluffy blanket and observes everything that is going on around him. He loves to meet new dogs, some are nice to him, some are not, but he is always hopeful they will show him kindness. When they arrive, he starts wagging his tail and whimpering in his crate as to say *Come sit next to me and be my friend.* As Logan's muscles and bones get healthier, more dogs are friendly to him.

Logan will go into the same training as Luna. He will be working with seniors and veterans. At times he can be a little jealous if he thinks Luna is getting more attention. One time she ran into the house so quickly she slammed her hip on the door. She banged it pretty hard and was struggling to walk. I started giving Luna leg massages and was very attentive as to how she was walking. Logan awoke from his nap, gently slid off the sofa and began to limp, pretending he hurt his leg too. He got a massage, but I know he faked his injury.

Much to my own surprise, I started allowing Logan to wear a red bandana like Luke. Logan and Luna wear bandanas when they know they are going someplace special. I had decided Logan would wear green because he has an Irish name. Every bandana that I gave him he destroyed once we got home. One day we were going to an event where his picture was going to be taken, I put on one of Luke's red bandana (I had kept all three of them) when we got home from event Logan would not allow me to take it off. He kept it on his neck for a couple of days unharmed. Logan has filled the void Luke left. He looks completely different from Luke, but he is my reminder to keep helping animals, that there is hope for those deemed hopeless.

Me

As for myself, I was fortunate to start a career at a young age. I have earned titles such as: accomplished, educated, goal-oriented, doctor, professor, and successful. But it was opening my home to animals in need that granted me the recognition of bright, happy and joyful! I have been told numerous times by friends that they considered me to be happier than they have ever seen me before.

My journey and story with my dogs will continue. I get as much as I can get done in a day but am prepared for delays along the way. My house is filled with more laughter than ever before. I have seen so many miracles through my career and spiritual transition that my faith in Jesus Christ is the strongest it has ever been. I have big dreams and goals for Love from Luke Dog Sanctuary. I believe they will all be accomplished in God's time. I have given up micromanaging every aspect of my life. I enjoy helping my dogs be able to serve their local community. They are frequently reminded that they have been blessed to be a blessing.

My dogs and I are the underdogs of the underdogs, with promising futures ahead of us. I am excited for the day Luna and Logan are officially ready to walk into the hospital and bring smiles to countless faces. I am grateful when individuals contact me because they have dogs with physical disabilities. They have shared that because of Logan and Luna they believe their dog can have a healthy happy life too, just a tad bit unique. There will be more foster dogs and Love from Luke books. Thanks again for showing your support and allowing us to share some of our stories with you, until next time - God Bless!

******

And the Angels Cried with Us

In the midst of editing this book, my world came to a sudden pause. On August 2, 2018, the animal rescue community lost a leader, mentor, and dear friend to many, Lori. I am sure everyone who knew Lori will remember exactly where they were when they received the news. My day was finished; I was in my bedroom looking for a movie to watch. I received a text from Ellie, all it said was "Lori is gone," with about 10 emoji crying faces.

Lori was an animal rescue guru to many. The founder of one of the dog rescues I volunteer with. She was kind, and always made time for me, regardless of how many animals she fostered and what she had going on in her own life. She was so focused on the well-being of animals that unless directly asked how she was feeling, there was no mention of her chemotherapy or that she had stage four cancer. In fact, very few people knew she was bravely battling cancer.

Instantly, I thought I will never hear her voice or the words, "Good job," or "Keep going, you're making great progress with your fosters," again. Occasionally, I would get a "Good job, kid," which I always got a kick out. Although Lori probably heard similar stories by everyone, she always got a good laugh hearing about how Chimayo would keep the younger and larger dogs in line. She really thought it was funny when he would take their toys away if they teased him. She would call me randomly just to offer words of encouragement with Luna and Lucy. She would say, "I can see the love in their eyes when they look at you."

I did not expect my reaction to be as severe as it was when I found out she passed. Instantly, tears burst out of my eyes, within seconds I was loudly sobbing. Chimayo came rushing over to me and started licking my tears away. I sat back on the bed as I hugged him and accepted his comfort. Logan, Luna, and Lucy heard me crying and started tapping their paws outside my bedroom door. I cannot remember a time I cried so hard. The sounds I was making must have scared them. Chimayo just leaned in on me and allowed me to cry into his fur until I calmed down.

When I thought I was done, I washed my face and left my bedroom to try and assure my other dogs, that it was okay. They did not understand what was wrong with me. Chimayo crawled up the top of my bed and placed his head on a pillow. Poor guy, I'm sure I gave him a headache.

When I stepped out of the bedroom, I had all three dogs looking up at my concerned and confused. They wanted to comfort me but did not know what to do. They had never seen me like this. While looking down at them I was suddenly blown away by the realization of all Lori had accomplished, my mind became overwhelmed and I was flooded with emotions. These three dogs were saved because of Lori and her team. She was the one who posted on social media seeking a foster for Lucy. She stayed in consistent contact with me while working with Lucy till a routine was created. No concern was too small for her to acknowledge. I thought about how my dogs bring happiness and laughter to so many. The week prior I was out with five friends. At least 45 minutes of our conversation was based on the mischief and the personalities of my dogs. My friends had a good laugh, the type that brings tears to your eyes because it's so hard.

Lori was humbly behind it all, but it was far more significant than just my group of friends and family. In the future, she will be a part of Logan and Luna bringing smiles to countless faces in hospitals. Not only, did she rescue over 5,000 dogs, but she improved an even larger amount of individual lives. I became emotional again realizing the far-reaching impact Lori had on so many. I finally understood what happens when a person lives out the calling and pursues the passion God has placed on their heart. What Lori founded was tearfully beautiful. I became aware of the magnificence just one person CAN create!

Lori met a special dog that she named Heidi, who ignited the spark in her to go into animal rescue in the early 2000's. Heidi passed away but was a great comfort to her during one of her fights against cancer. In Heidi's honor, she changed the lives of countless dogs, the people who fostered the dogs from her rescue, the families who adopted the dogs, their friends, children, the list is infinite. Lori's life demonstrated how small acts of kindness can amplify into something larger, and more wonderful than most could ever imagine.

I looked at the dogs I have because of her and her team, and remembered just how many individuals were involved in each of the rescues. I realized how everything came together, and the importance of each person's role. My sobbing started again. I slid down against the wall and sat with my dogs in the hallway outside my bedroom. Logan and Luna sat down next to me on the floor. Just like Chimayo, they kissed my face and allowed me to hug them. Lucy came into the hallway, with a concerned look on her face, and laid down about two feet away from me. She was doing her best to comfort me. I am sure I scared her, but she loved me enough to understand I would never hurt her. That night I was the one in pain and needed comforting. What an awesome fur family Lori blessed me with. I was in awe that Lori's love of dogs did this for over 5,000 families throughout the United States.

When I finally stopped crying, I went outside to get some fresh air. My dogs were staying close in case I needed their support again. I texted a few people to tell them about Lori. Like many I was too upset to hold a conversation. I posted on social media explaining one of my mentors in dog rescue had passed away. Animal rescue groups from all over the country posted condolences to the loss of Lori. Countless families posted pictures of the dogs they adopted through Lori's rescue. Many of these dogs were special needs, dogs that were blind, deaf, physically disabled or had to overcome horrific physical abuse. Every picture posted regardless of the dogs past showed them in their new life with huge smiles on their faces. Lori was the originator of these smiles. She mentored all her volunteers who needed to learn how to effectively work with special needs dogs. Not only did these dogs learn to smile, but they brought smiles many others who encountered them. Everyone who knew Lori understood we lost an earth angel. Lori was a courageous warrior, who bravely fought and beat cancer four times before Jesus called her home. Yet, all of us left felt lost and empty without our leader.

As I was sitting in the backyard under the stars, I received a text from a friend who adopted one of the dogs I had fostered. She had also volunteered with the rescue before. She asked if I knew what would happen with the rescue. I told her I didn't know because everything had happened a few hours before my post. I explained I was going to continue working on my vision with dog rescue and Love from Luke. She also explained that her dog was going through training to assist children in the school system. Amazing, another dog that was going to help many that was first helped by Lori.

As I sat mesmerized by the infinite list of happiness Lori brought into the world it started to rain. It was a decent Florida downpour, but it was a quiet and gentle. It smelled like spring versus the heavy tropical storm type rain we get in August. I stood in the entrance of my doorway looking outside and thought, God's angels are crying for the ones mourning Lori tonight.

Foolishly, in tears, I text Ellie asking if she was okay. No, she was not okay, none of us were okay, our hearts were broken worse than we could have imagined. What a silly message to send I thought to myself. The evening of August 2, 2018, most of my friends in the animal rescue community were grieving. About four hours later Ellie returned my text, *"No, I am not okay, but we will carry on in her memory."*

When I read those words, I realized we physically lost Lori. She held on as long as she could. She fought against cancer on-and-off for 16 years of her life. She was a fearless warrior, humble about all she did for dogs, but would quickly tell someone where to go if they attempted to mess with a dog she rescued. Lori was so special she left her fire, drive and immense compassion inside our hearts. We as a rescue community, although hurting and sad would continue because of our love for her. The one-on-one time she spent advising and mentoring us was enough. There was a greater drive than ever to help wounded and abused animals. Rescuing animals was not going to stop because our leader went to heaven. It was going to continue because we loved our leader and this is what she wanted us to do.

The next day was hard. I would check Lori's social media sites and read posts from other rescues, her volunteers and people who had adopted from her. People started posting pictures of rainbows they saw, angel and dog shaped clouds, and beautiful sunsets claiming it was Lori looking down on us from heaven, reminding us to keep going. This may sound ridiculous to some, but we needed this. The painstaking grief of losing Lori caused many of us to stumble and wobble for a bit. Our crying caused us to momentarily lose our voices, when her goal for us was to continue to be the voices for the voiceless. We needed to see these angel and dog shape clouds. We needed these extra beautiful rainbows and sunsets to prevent us from falling and becoming speechless. For us, these were signs from Lori, to keep going in her honor, in Heidi's honor, in Luke's, and Adam's honor, and for all the special dogs that have softened our hearts forever.

The sorrow of losing Lori is still too fresh to discuss without crying. At this moment, when I start to talk about her, I burst into tears, and my eyes burn from crying so much. There will come a time when I can compose myself, and share all that Lori has done in a dignified manner. I know that day will come. There are *funny, happy memories, adventures and stories of triumph that will be shared.*

Much like what I learned with Luke, just because we are hurting does not mean we will stop. There are tails that need to learn to wag, faces that need to smile, hearts that need to mend, and compassion that needs to be spread. Now there is a fire in many hearts greater than ever before. This all started with one dog and a fearless woman who boldly answered the calling God placed on her heart, a courageous woman, who pursued her passion to help the less fortunate, and never let anyone stand in her way. Lori, this is all because of you! Leadership that inspires and changes a person's heart is rare, and you possessed that gift. Thank you, my friend, leader, and mentor, thank you!

Heart Shaped Cloud that I saw when I went outside after writing about Lori.

Melissa and her best friend of 14 years, Chimayo

Melissa currently resides in Florida. She is originally from Milford, Massachusetts. From a young age, Melissa was always bringing animals home in need of rehabilitation and love. If it had a heartbeat she cared for it: dogs, cats, birds, squirrels, and lizards to list a few. Melissa continues helping animals today. The underdogs and the dogs deemed unadoptable have a special place in her heart. Prior to full-time rescue, Melissa was a college professor and cultural scientist. She earned a Doctorate in International Business.

Website: www.lovefromluke.com

Facebook: www.facebook.com/loveluke888

Instagram: Loveluke888

YouTube: LovefromLukeDogSanctuary

www.ingramcontent.com/pod-product-compliance
Lightning Source LLC
LaVergne TN
LVHW051515070426
835507LV00023B/3131